DAYBOOK

OF CRITICAL READING AND WRITING

daybook, n. a book in which the events of the day are recorded; specif. a journal or diary

THE AUTHORS
* Laura Robb
* Michael F. Opitz
* Ellin Oliver Keene

Great Source Education Group
A division of Houghton Mifflin Company
Wilmington, Massachusetts

D0719904

THE AUTHORS

✳ **Laura Robb** has more than forty years of classroom experience in grades 4 through 8. Robb also coaches teachers in grades K to 12 in school districts in her home state of Virginia, New York, and Michigan and speaks at conferences throughout the country. Author of more than fifteen books for teachers, Robb's latest title is *Teaching Reading: A Complete Resource for Grades Four and Up* (Scholastic, 2006). For Great Source, Robb has developed, with other authors, *Reading Advantage, Writing Advantage, and Reader's Handbook* for grades 3 to 8.

✳ **Michael F. Opitz** is Professor of Reading at the University of Northern Colorado, where he teaches graduate and undergraduate literacy courses. He is the author or coauthor of several books including *Diagnosis and Improvement in Reading Instruction,* 5th ed. (Allyn & Bacon, 2007), *Books and Beyond* (Heinemann, 2006), *Listen, Hear!* (Heinemann, 2005), and *Goodbye Round Robin* (Heinemann, 1998) as well as the reading programs *Afterschool Achievers: Reading Club* (Great Source, 2004) and *Literacy By Design* (Harcourt, 2007).

✳ **Ellin Oliver Keene** has been a classroom teacher, staff developer, and adjunct professor of reading and writing. For sixteen years, she directed staff development initiatives at the Denver-based Public Education & Business Coalition. She served as Deputy Director and Director of Literacy and Staff Development for the Cornerstone Project at the University of Pennsylvania for four years. Ellin is co-author of *Mosaic of Thought: Teaching Comprehension in a Readers' Workshop* (Heinemann, 1997), the second edition of which will be released in 2007. She is also the author of *To Understand* (Heinemann, 2007) and *Assessing Comprehension Thinking Strategies* (Shell Educational Books, 2006).

REVIEWERS

Susan Dinges
Mt. Olive Public Schools
Budd Lake, NJ

Fran Ellis
Lake Stevens School District
Lake Stevens, WA

Brook E. Meiler
Norman Public Schools
Norman, OK

EDITORIAL: Ruth Rothstein and Sue Paro
DESIGN AND PRODUCTION: AARTPACK, Inc.

Printed in the United States of America

International Standard Book Number 13: 978-0-669-54979-9

International Standard Book Number 10: 0-669-54979-7

1 2 3 4 5 6 7 8 9 10 - VH - 12 11 10 09 08 07

Contents

Focus / Skill		Selection / Author	

High LIGHTER

NEW GEO...RA...ES

Becoming an Active Reader

If your goal is to play the drums or be part of a basketball team, you need to practice every day to reach your goal. What do you practice? You practice specific skills and strategies to help you become an expert at playing your sport or instrument.

Reading is just like sports or music—you need to practice every day to develop and improve your skills.

The strategy lessons in this Daybook will build your reading skill and power. In each unit, you'll interact with texts by making connections, asking questions, determining importance, visualizing, making inferences, and synthesizing. By actively using these strategies, you'll find that you understand, remember, and enjoy more of what you read.

North Star, 118°, 122-122*
Nose, 84

When you read, look for ideas and details that remind you of things you already know. This is called **making connections**. Making connections with a text will help you better understand and remember what you read. Connections can be made between texts and your own feelings and experience, other texts, online resources, movies, or issues facing your community or the world.

Practice making connections with *The Street Sweeper*, a short story. Mark the text by underlining phrases or sentences that remind you of things you already know. Explain your connections in the **Response Notes**. An example is shown.

Response Notes

I would've brought the money to a bank.

from The Street Sweeper

by Ruthilde Kronberg and Patricia C. McKissack

A poor peasant lost his crops to bad weather three years in a row. Because he could not feed his family any longer, he sent his wife and his daughter back to his wife's parents and went into the city to become a street sweeper. Hoping to save as much money as possible, he worked long, hard hours and spent almost nothing on himself.

When he had a small sum of money saved, he became afraid that thieves might steal it. <u>He decided to bring it to a rich jeweler who had given him an extra job now and then. The peasant asked the jeweler to safeguard his money.</u> In his innocence he thought that a man with so much wealth must be trustworthy.

The jeweler was more than willing to take the money. He promised to keep it in a safe place, and at the end of each month the street sweeper added more of his hard-earned pennies.

Five years passed, and the street sweeper decided he had saved up enough to go home. With a happy heart he went to the jeweler's house and asked for his money.

Ask questions before, during, and after reading. Asking questions helps keep you interested in the reading because you search for the answers. Through questioning, your thinking becomes clearer.

As you read, ask questions about what will happen next, why a person makes a certain decision, how a character feels, or how an invention will help you and others. Sometimes readers question the author directly to figure out the ideas that the author is trying to send.

As you continue reading *The Street Sweeper,* underline or circle parts of the text that raise questions or cause you to question the author. Write your questions in the **Response Notes.**

from The Street Sweeper *continued*

The jeweler looked at him in amazement and said, "My good man, what are you talking about? I've never seen you before in my life."

"How can you say that?" demanded the street sweeper. "You have known me for five years. I came to you at the end of each month and brought you my money for safekeeping."

"Do you have a witness?" sneered the jeweler. "If you do, bring him to my house. If you don't, you do not have a leg to stand on. Now leave my shop before I call the police."

"I did not think a witness would be necessary" pleaded the poor street sweeper. "I thought I could trust you."

"Do not bother me any longer. God only knows what you did with your money," said the jeweler. "Now leave! You are wasting my time."

"I won't leave until you give me my money," cried the poor street sweeper.

The jeweler rang a bell, and immediately two burly servants entered and threw the street sweeper out into the street. There he sat with tears streaming down his face.

Response Notes

Why does the author use the word *burly?* Maybe he wants me to imagine big, mean-looking servants.

As you read, you pause at times to **determine which details and ideas are important.** You use your background knowledge, opinions, and purpose for reading to help you make your choices. Your choices may be different from someone else's.

As you read the next part of *The Street Sweeper*, notice what the characters say. Underline the most important sentences, phrases, and words. Explain your choices in the **Response Notes.**

Response Notes

The little girl reminds her mother to help. The story would end differently if the mother chose not to help.

from The Street Sweeper *continued*

Just then a carriage drove by. Inside sat a woman and her little daughter.

"Mommy," said the little girl. "Why is that man crying?"

"Hush," said the mother. "I am sure he does not want us to know why he is crying."

"But, Mommy, you always say we should help people who are sad," the child said.

To satisfy her, the mother asked the driver to stop the carriage. "Forgive me for bothering you," she said to the street sweeper. "My daughter insists that I find out what is troubling you. Perhaps I can help."

"I have lost five years of my life," said the street sweeper. Then he told her his sad story.

"I have heard others say that the jeweler is a scoundrel," replied the woman. "Let's see if we can't get your money back. Tomorrow morning I will go and speak to him. Sweep the street in front of his house and watch for my arrival. About ten minutes after you see me enter the house, come inside and ask for your money. Do not mention what happened today, and pray that my plan works."

The street sweeper began to pray as he had never prayed before.

When you read, certain words and phrases create **sensory images** in your mind. A sensory image can make you feel as though you see, hear, feel, taste, or smell something. These images help you **visualize** and better understand what you're reading.

As you read this passage from *The Street Sweeper*, underline words and phrases that create sensory images. In the **Response Notes**, write about or draw the images you see and feel while reading.

from The Street Sweeper *continued*

The woman went home and put her most precious jewels into a jewelry box. The following morning she went to the jeweler. <u>She showed him her jewels</u>. "My family and I just moved into this city," she explained. "But your reputation as an expert on fine jewels has already reached my ears, and I came to you for advice. My husband went on a business trip to a city far away. Yesterday a messenger arrived to say that my husband wants me to join him because his business will take longer than he thought. But he forgot to send instructions about what to do with my jewels, and I do not know what to do. If I take them along, they might be stolen. If I leave them at home, they might be stolen too."

"If I were you, I would not take them on a journey," said the jeweler. "<u>I have a burglar-proof safe, and I would be glad to keep them for you.</u>"

"I was hoping you would say that," replied the woman. "But how will we go about it? I hardly know anyone in this town. Where would I find someone to witness our transaction?"

"There is no need for that," replied the jeweler. "You can trust me. I will return your jewels to you the minute you come back from your journey."

Response Notes

I imagine a huge diamond ring.

I can almost hear the dishonesty in his voice!

Authors don't include every possible detail when they write. They purposely leave out bits of information that they expect you to **infer,** or figure out. In a text, look for clues that reveal hidden details the author doesn't state. When you combine these clues with your own thoughts to create new information, you are **making an inference.** An inference can be a prediction, a conclusion, or an interpretation. Making inferences will deepen your understanding of a text.

As you read the next section of *The Street Sweeper,* infer what the characters are secretly thinking. Underline sentences and phrases that spark your inferences. Write your inferences in the **Response Notes.**

Response Notes

The woman is secretly thinking that the jeweler is NOT honest.

The Street Sweeper *continued*

The woman looked at him as if she were trying to make up her mind what to do.

Just then the poor street sweeper entered and said, "Sir, I decided to go back to my family. Would you please be so kind as to give me the money you kept for me?"

For a brief moment the jeweler looked angry. But then he smiled wickedly and said, "Of course." He opened his safe, and as he gave the street sweeper his money, he said to the woman, "People come to me all the time and ask me to safeguard their money."

"I am glad there are still some honest people in this world," replied the woman. "I have made up my mind. I shall leave my jewels with you." She closed her jewelry box and was just about to hand it to the jeweler when the door opened and her maid came running inside, saying, "My lady! A second messenger arrived while you were gone and said that your husband's plans had to be changed. He will arrive within a few hours."

"What better thing could happen to me!" replied the woman. She turned to the jeweler. "Thank you, my dear friend, for offering to keep my jewels." She bowed and left while the jeweler gnashed his teeth.

CLOSED

As you read and reread a text, your thoughts and ideas change. You learn new information that affects how you think or feel about a piece. As your thoughts and ideas evolve, you **synthesize**, or create, new understandings. Often these new understandings are big ideas or themes the author is trying to get across.

When you finish *The Street Sweeper*, reread your Response Notes for the entire selection. Think about the twists and turns your mind took along the way. Then review all your thoughts and feelings about the piece to synthesize some big ideas or themes. Write your big ideas or themes in the **Response Notes**. Then share and discuss them with a partner.

The Street Sweeper *continued*

The following day the clever woman invited all her friends and the street sweeper to her home. After everyone had eaten heartily, she told the story of the treacherous jeweler. Her friends passed the story on, and soon the jeweler was the most despised person in the city. In time he had to close his shop and leave because no one would associate with a man who stole money from the poorest of the poor.

The street sweeper returned to his family. With the money he had saved, he was able to restock his little farm, and they had enough to eat for the rest of their lives. ❖

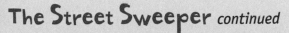

Response Notes

Cheating can come back to haunt you. Sometimes strangers can help a lot.

The Best Story Ever

nerd

Making Connections

Imagine this: You're visiting your cousin in another city. Your cousin says, "Let's get a hoagie." You have no idea what he's talking about, but you go along and hope for the best. You get to a restaurant. Out front, there's a big picture of a turkey sandwich on a long roll with cheese, lettuce, and tomato. The sign says "Joe's Famous Hoagies." Now you get it! A hoagie is just another name for a sub or a hero or a grinder. You may not realize it, but you just used your own experience to **make a connection.**

In this unit, you will connect with events and with characters' thoughts, words, and actions as they **follow their dreams.** People and characters who have sought after their dreams can inspire and teach you.

15

When you read, you make connections between what happens in the text and what has happened in your own life. **Making connections** helps you understand what you are reading by comparing it with something you already know. The more connections you make, the more meaning you will get out of your reading.

This passage is from the novel *The Young Man and the Sea*. In this section, Skiff goes deep-sea fishing alone, without enough food or equipment. In the **Response Notes**, you will see how one reader made connections with the text. Mark any text that reminds you of something you already know.

from The Young Man and the Sea by Rodman Philbrick

Response Notes

When you hear a <u>foghorn</u> you're supposed to signal back. That way the other boat gets an idea where you are and steers away. Trouble is, I never thought to bring along a horn. Didn't even think there might be fog, which is really dumb because I know better. Maybe that's what the dream was telling me about not having a voice. Don't matter now, there's nothing I can do but listen.

Blaaaaaat.

Big old foghorn seems to be getting closer. I can hear a boat engine thumping. Then it seems to be going away and the engine gets fainter and fainter and the horn sounds smaller and then the wake comes through and rocks me like a baby in a cradle and I'm alone again inside the fog.

"How long did you sleep, you reckon?"

That's me talking out loud to myself. Got no good answer because another thing I forgot to bring along is a wristwatch. Figured I'd know what time of day it was from the sun, but the fog has come on thick again and I can't tell where the sun is, except it feels like I slept for a long time, so it might be afternoon now.

"Skiff Beaman, you are a darn fool."

Response Notes (margin):

I've heard a foghorn.

It's loud.

I know that feeling!

I hate it when I get myself into a mess.

There. Almost feels good to say it. To speak the truth out loud. Only a darn fool would do what I did. Go to sea in a ten-foot plywood skiff without a thought in my head but catch-a-big-fish. Like there was no room in my brain for what happens if there's fog, or you can't find the fish, or you can't hit the fish even if you find them. Turns out I found the fish all right, but it don't matter because I'm not big enough or strong enough to hit one with the harpoon. So here I am thirty miles out to sea in a blind fog with nothing but a few peanut butter and jelly sandwiches and a jug of water. Oh, and a compass in case I decide to give up and go home. Which I ain't ready for, not yet.

He doesn't have a lot of food.

Why bother? Home is Dad on the TV couch and a boat with no engine and a rich kid laughing while he cuts my traps. Home is where my mom don't live anymore except she's still there somehow, in all the rooms of our little house, me and my dad missing her something fierce and not wanting to give up how much it hurts because that would be like forgetting. Home is a rickety old dock and an outhouse with a half-moon cut in the door, and the bright orange flowers my mom called "outhouse lilies." Home is where everything happens, good or bad, except it's been mostly bad lately. ❖

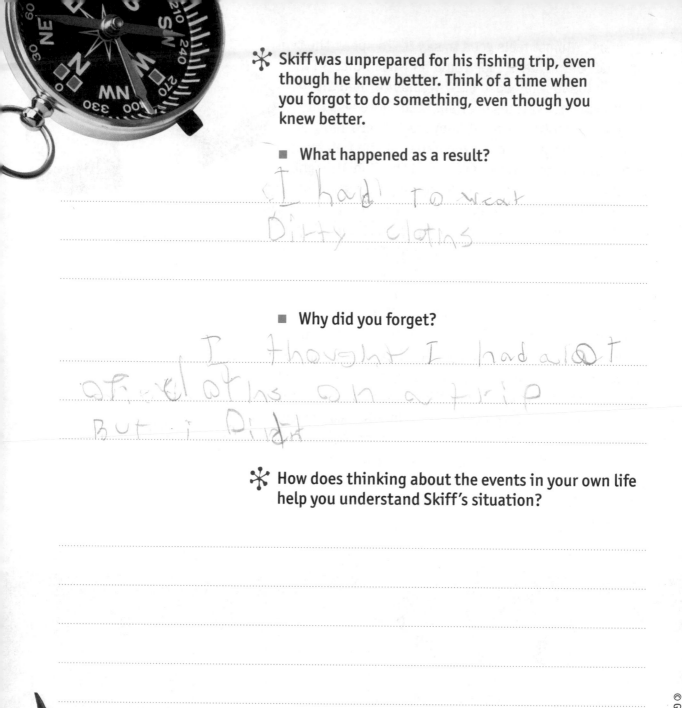

❋ Skiff was unprepared for his fishing trip, even though he knew better. Think of a time when you forgot to do something, even though you knew better.

■ **What happened as a result?**

I had to weat
Ditty clotns

■ **Why did you forget?**

I thought I had alot
of cloths on a trip
But i Didtt

❋ How does thinking about the events in your own life help you understand Skiff's situation?

✳ Make a list of everything you would need for a fishing trip similar to the one Skiff took.

- compass, water, food
- watch, horn, fishing, gear
- Boat, heat

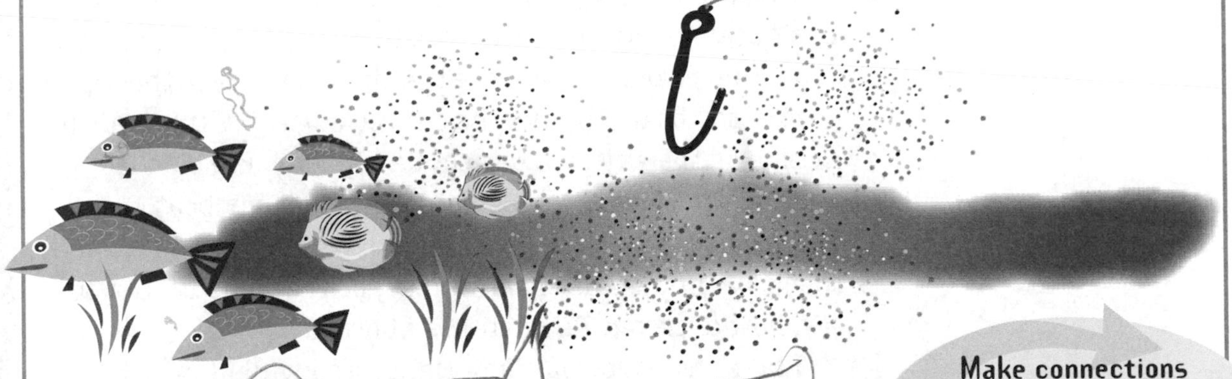

Make connections with the text to help you understand what you're reading.

Does a book you're reading ever remind you of another book you know? A connection like that will help you understand and remember both books.

Skiff's adventure continues below. As you read, think about stories you know that include similar characters, people, or events. Underline details that remind you of other texts. In the **Response Notes**, write connections you make between this story and other texts you have read.

Response Notes

from The Young Man and the Sea by Rodman Philbrick

So I'm lying there in the bottom of my little skiff, munching on a sticky sandwich and feeling sorry for myself when the whoosh comes by.

Whoosh.

There it is again. Sound of something slicing through the water. Not far away, either. Right on the other side of the plywood hull, a few feet from my head.

Whoosh.

Careful, I tell myself. Sit up slow. Don't rock the boat. Don't scare away whatever it is that's making that sound.

I sit up real slow. And see the tip of a fin over the top edge of the boat. Fin like the curved edge of a knife. A fin as blue as the sky on a perfect day in May. Big blue fin making the whoosh as a giant fish circles my boat.

Harpoon is lying along the seats with the tip out over the bow. I know what I want to do, but can I do it? Got to try. Now or never. No mistakes allowed.

I take the harpoon in my right hand while I'm still sitting down, facing the back of the boat. Keep hold of it while I ever so quiet stand up and turn around and face the front. Quiet now, quiet as a mouse. I stand on the seat without making a sound and look over the side into the dark, wet eye of a giant bluefin tuna, close enough to touch, and so alive, I swear I can hear his heart beating.

I'm looking down on the biggest fish I ever seen in my life. Bigger than me. Bigger than my boat. Bigger than any tuna I ever seen brought into the dock.

I got the harpoon raised but I don't dare move, not until it's perfect, not until I'm ready to strike.

I swear the giant fish is looking at the boat. Like maybe it wants to know if this is where the chum comes from that brings the mackerel it likes to eat. Can it still pick up on the scent of the bait I was cutting up and tossing over? Is that it? What's it thinking? Why is it circling my boat? Or is it circling me? Curious about a small boy with a long stick in his hand.

I never realized how much bigger a bluefin tuna looks when it's alive in the ocean instead of dead on the dock. I can feel the power as it swims by, making the boat rock with the *whoosh-whoosh-whoosh* of its giant tail shoving it through the water easy as can be. Man on the dock said the tail can move faster than the eye can see, but this one is going slow, gliding along as easy as can be. Almost like its showing off. *Look at me, you puny human. Look at my big bad self, you never seen nothing so awesome as me.*

✳ **What does this scene make you think of? Jot down a quick thought.**

The big bluefin is so amazing and so beautiful, I almost forget what I need to do. Almost but not quite. My dad used to call it "getting froze up." Man out in the pulpit of a tuna boat, he's waiting for hours for a chance to throw and when the chance finally comes, he can't do it. Like the fish sort of hypnotizes you into not throwing the harpoon.

Froze up. Come to think of it, that's sort of what happened to Dad when Mom died. Except he ain't on a tuna boat, he's on the TV couch. Stuck on how miserable he feels.

Never mind your father and the couch, Skiffy. Concentrate on the fish!

She's right. There's plenty of time to worry about my dad later. So I wrap both hands around the shaft of the harpoon and plunge it straight down at the biggest part of the fish. Straight down with all my might. Straight down so hard and fast, I fall halfway out of the boat and my face is an inch from the water and I'm looking down and I don't see nothing.

Fish disappeared. Gone in the blink of an eye.

Had my chance and missed. Again.

I groan and roll over and rub my knee where I bumped it and then I fetch the harpoon and pull it into the boat. That's when I notice the barb is missing. Must have come loose when I fell down. Great. Harpoon without a barb is just a long stick. Then I remember the barb is attached to the keg line, so all I got to do is pull the line in and put the barb back on the harpoon.

Who knows? If I drift around for another hundred years or so, I might find another fish as big as the one that got away. Anyhow, I put my hand on the line and give it a tug and then a weird thing happens. The line slips through my hands.

Line is running out of the tub, over the side of the boat, and straight down into the water.

For a moment I can't make my brain figure out what that means, line running out of the boat, and then I stand up and shout, "FISH ON! FISH ON!" at the top of my lungs.

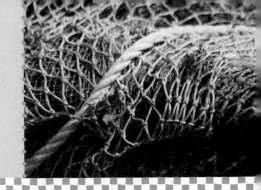

Nobody around to hear me, so it's like I'm shouting to myself, to make me believe what happened. I hit the big fish! He's got the barb in his back and he's diving deep, dragging line out of the tub. I'm so excited, I fall down again and crack another shin but I don't even care that it hurts because I got a fish on the line. ❖

✳ The author uses the term "froze up" in two different ways. Find the two ways on page 22. Then fill in the chart with your thoughts.

What does Skiff's dad mean by "getting froze up"?	What does Skiff mean by "froze up"?	How have you experienced "getting froze up"?

✳ What other books, stories, movies, or articles does this selection make you think of? Fill in the chart with your thoughts.

Name of book, story, movie, or article	What connections do you make between the two?

Making connections between texts will help you better understand them.

A character trait describes what a person is like. Examples of traits are *shy*, *brave*, and *generous*. Do you have any character traits in common with Harry Houdini, the famous magician? You might be surprised.

As you read this biographical sketch, try to make personal connections. Underline words or phrases that show Houdini's character traits. In the **Response Notes**, write comments about the connections you make to them.

from The American Story
by Jennifer Armstrong

Beginning in the 1880s, hundreds of thousands of Jews from eastern Europe began flocking to America, the Golden Land. Among those in search of new lives and new luck were the Weiss family from Budapest, Hungary. Ehrich "Ehrie" Weiss, the son, was a strong, athletic boy with a flair for wrestling attention to the ground and standing on its neck. By the time he was a teenager, he was ready to go into show business as a magician, and he took the name of his idol, the great French magician Jean Eugène Robert-Houdin, for his stage name. Ehrie Weiss became Harry Houdini.

His stock-in-trade was escapes. No handcuffs could bind him. Straitjackets were no match for Houdini. Before electrified audiences, he freed himself from ropes, chains, locks, sealed containers, boxes, tanks of water. Upside down, naked, manacled, he dropped off bridges into icy rivers to the astonishment of crowds, only to pop up to the surface, free and smiling. He was a sensation, the toast of Europe and the American vaudeville stage.

But no matter how death-defying his act, there was always an imitator waiting in the wings. Houdini's acts became more and more dangerous. In 1912, he was offered a job at Hammerstein's Roof Garden in New York City at the kingly sum of $1,000 a week. He was determined to come up with a trick for his debut that no paltry copycat could steal.

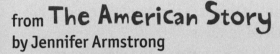

Response Notes

One morning New Yorkers read the following advertisement with gasps of amazement: "Houdini, securely handcuffed and leg ironed, will be placed in a heavy packing case, which will be nailed and roped, then encircled by steel bands, firmly nailed. Two hundred pounds of iron weights will then be lashed to this box containing HOUDINI. The box will then be THROWN INTO THE RIVER. Houdini will undertake to release himself whilst submerged under water."

Surely even the great Houdini wasn't up to this challenge! Crowds of curiosity seekers packed the East River pier that afternoon as Houdini's assistants readied the crate. Grim-visaged Houdini, in a wool bathing costume, was preparing to enter the packing case of doom when the police arrived in force.

Jumping into the East River from the pier was not allowed, not even for the great Houdini, they announced with a flourish of nightsticks.

But if handcuffs and straitjackets couldn't get the better of Houdini, neither could New York's finest. A nearby tugboat was called into service. Houdini and a babbling escort of newspapermen clambered on, and the boat made its way into the harbor.

Then—handcuffs locked, leg irons locked, the escape artist extraordinaire was placed in the box, the box was secured and weighted, and lowered into the water. Bug-eyed with anticipation, champing at their damp cigars, the newspapermen hauled their watches out of their pockets and began the count.

A mere fifty-seven seconds later, Houdini bobbed up like a cork, scarcely breathing hard. The press corps on the boat went wild. When Houdini repeated the stunt at Hammerstein's that night, the audience was spellbound.

Houdini asked for his first week's salary to be paid in gold. He took it home to his mother and poured it into her lap. The Hungarian immigrant had conquered America, the Golden Land. ✤

✳ Identify two character traits Houdini has. Can you connect to them? Explain.

his a Brave, Dreamer

✳ Houdini had a dream that shaped his life. What is your dream? Explain how you will achieve it and how it could shape your life.

I won't to be a Asttohaut,

Making connections to a character can help you understand a text.

When you read a **biography**, you're reading about a real person. You may discover that you and the person are alike or different.

American artist Grant Wood is the subject of the biography *Artist in Overalls*. In this passage from the book, you'll read about Grant's childhood and his love of drawing. As you read, try to make connections with Grant and his early life. What experiences have you had that are similar to Grant's? The more connections you make, the better you will understand the subject. Underline sentences and phrases you can relate to, and write connections you make in the **Response Notes**.

Response Notes

from Artist in Overalls by John Duggleby

Grant was a shy boy. More than anything else, he liked to draw. He drew whenever he could, using charred black sticks pulled carefully from the cooking stove and white cardboard torn from cracker boxes. That was all he had. In 1898 fancy drawing supplies were only a dream for a farm boy whose house didn't even have electricity.

Everything Grant saw around him ended up on those cracker boxes. He drew houses, barns, trees, cows, cats—but most of all, he drew chickens. They were like pets to him, the way they pecked at the cookies he shared as he sat outside his house. His favorites were his mother's Plymouth Rock hens, with their black and white feathers arranged in neat crescent-moon shapes. He drew them every way possible—sitting on giant piles of eggs, clucking, fighting.

Once in a while, Grant's parents examined his drawings. His father solemnly peered at a hen as though he were judging it at the county fair. "That's a lot of eggs for one hen to lay," was all he said.

Grant's father was very serious. He felt that everything should have a definite purpose. Drawing would never get the crops planted or harvested. Why couldn't Grant be more like his brother, Frank, who was four years older? Frank was so good at tinkering with machinery that he could already fix some of the farm tools.

Grant's mother was more encouraging. She thought his interest in art was just fine, and she admired his talent. She believed that someday he would be famous. But others weren't so sure.

At the one-room schoolhouse he attended, Grant was often daydreaming when Miss Linden, the teacher, called on him. And by mid-morning, he was usually squirming in his desk like the snakes he chased outside. Sometimes Miss Linden just gave up, and told Grant to go outside and keep himself busy for a while. Grant waited for these moments.

Outside, everything was different. Grant sometimes fumbled for answers in geography or arithmetic, but he never missed anything going on around him. Like a sponge, he absorbed even the tiniest details of everything he saw. As he lay in a nearby meadow, he would gaze at the crisp white schoolhouse. In back of it were two neat little outhouses where the boys and girls went to the bathroom. In front was a scraggly young tree. To young Grant, the schoolyard looked like a stage, the way it rose suddenly from surrounding fields of corn. In the distance, the haze on a wooded grove shaped the trees into green balloons. It was the perfect place for a daydream.

One day, Grant began to think about "The Midnight Ride of Paul Revere," a poem his mother had read to him a few days earlier. When the United States was struggling for independence from England in the Revolutionary War, Revere saw enemy soldiers approaching. He galloped his horse through the streets of local villages shouting, "The British are coming! The British are coming!"

In Grant's imagination, the story changed to "The Midnight Ride of Grant Wood." He charged into Anamosa, the nearest town, to warn of a cyclone approaching. Everyone hailed him as a hero. He tried his daydream in real life by dashing into the schoolhouse with his awful warning. After Miss Linden saw that there was no cyclone, she rewarded Grant's imagination with a spanking he never forgot. ❖

✳ **What do you know about young Grant Wood? What was he like?**

What he did:

he DraWed
alot

How he felt:

good

young Grant Wood

How others felt about him:

not to good

What I think about him:

he was a Day Dreamer

✳ **How have your experiences been similar to Grant's?**

✳ Grant likes to creat art. His brother, Frank, likes to fix machines. With which brother do you connect with more?

....

....

....

....

✳ How does "making connections" get you more involved with reading? How does this help you remember and understand a text?

....

....

....

....

....

The more connections you make with characters and people, the more you will understand them.

Looking at others' lives can help you understand your own life. As you meet new characters, ask yourself, "How is this character like me or different from me? Would I ever behave like this character?" Connections like these will help you get a better sense of who the characters are and who you are.

The following passage is from the novel *Esperanza Rising* by Pam Muñoz Ryan. As you read, underline Esperanza's thoughts. Compare and contrast Esperanza's thoughts, words, and actions with your own. Write thoughts, questions, and comments in the **Response Notes**.

Response Notes

from Esperanza Rising by Pam Muñoz Ryan

A few days before her birthday, Esperanza begged Miguel to drive her to the foothills before sunrise. There was something she wanted to do. She woke in the dark and tiptoed from the cabin.

They followed the dirt road that headed east and parked when they could go no farther.

In the gray light, they could see a small footpath to a plateau.

When they got to the top, Esperanza looked out over the valley. The cool, almost-morning air filled her senses. Below, she could see the white roofs of the cabins in straight rows, the fields beginning to take form, and over the eastern mountains, a hopeful brightening.

She bent over and touched the grass. It was cool but dry. She lay down on her stomach and patted the ground next to her. "Miguel, did you know that if you lie on the ground and stay very still, you can feel the earth's heart beating?"

He looked at her skeptically.

She patted the ground again.

Then he lay down as she was, facing her.

"Will this happen soon, Esperanza?"

"*Aguántate tantito y la fruta caerá en tu mano.* Wait a little while and the fruit will fall into your hand."

He smiled and nodded.

They were still.

She watched Miguel watching her.

And then she felt it. Beginning softly. A gentle thumping, repeating itself. Then stronger. She heard it, too. *Shoomp. Shoomp. Shoomp.* The earth's heartbeat. Just like she had felt it that day with Papa.

Miguel smiled and she knew that he felt it, too.

The sun peeked over the rim of a distant ridge, bursting the dawn onto the waiting fields. She felt its warmth washing over her and turned on her back and faced the sky, staring into the clouds now tinged with pink and orange.

As the sun rose, Esperanza began to feel as if she rose with it. Floating again, like that day on the mountain, when she first arrived in the valley. She closed her eyes, and this time she did not career out of control. Instead, she glided above the earth, unafraid. She let herself be lifted into the sky, and she knew that she would not slip away. She knew that she would never lose Papa or El Rancho de las Rosas, or Abuelita or Mama, no matter what happened. It was as Carmen, the egg woman, had said on the train. She had her family, a garden full of roses, her faith, and the memories of those who had gone before her. But now, she had even more than that, and it carried her up, as on the wings of the phoenix. She soared with the anticipation of dreams she never knew she could have, of learning English, of supporting her family, of someday buying a tiny house. Miguel had been right about never giving up, and she had been right, too, about rising above those who held them down.

She hovered high above the valley, its basin surrounded by the mountains. She swooped over Papa's rose blooms, buoyed by rosehips that remembered all the beauty they had seen. She waved at Isabel and Abuelita, walking barefoot in the vineyards, wearing grapevine wreaths in their hair. She saw Mama, sitting on a blanket, a cacophony of color that covered an acre of zigzag rows.

She saw Marta and her mother walking in an almond grove, holding hands. Then she flew over a river, a

thrusting torrent that cut through the mountains. And there, in the middle of the wilderness, was a girl in a blue silk dress and a boy with his hair slicked down, eating mangoes on a stick, carved to look like exotic flowers, sitting on a grassy bank, on the same side of the river.

Esperanza reached for Miguel's hand and found it, and even though her mind was soaring to infinite possibilities, his touch held her heart to the earth. ❖

✳ What was Esperanza's dream?

✳ How were you able to connect with Esperanza's dream?

Idea from selection	My connection with the idea

✳ Think about Esperanza's dream and how it connects with your life. Write a letter to Esperanza. In your letter, tell her how her dream is similar to and different from yours.

Dear Esperanza,

....

....

....

....

....

....

....

Your friend,

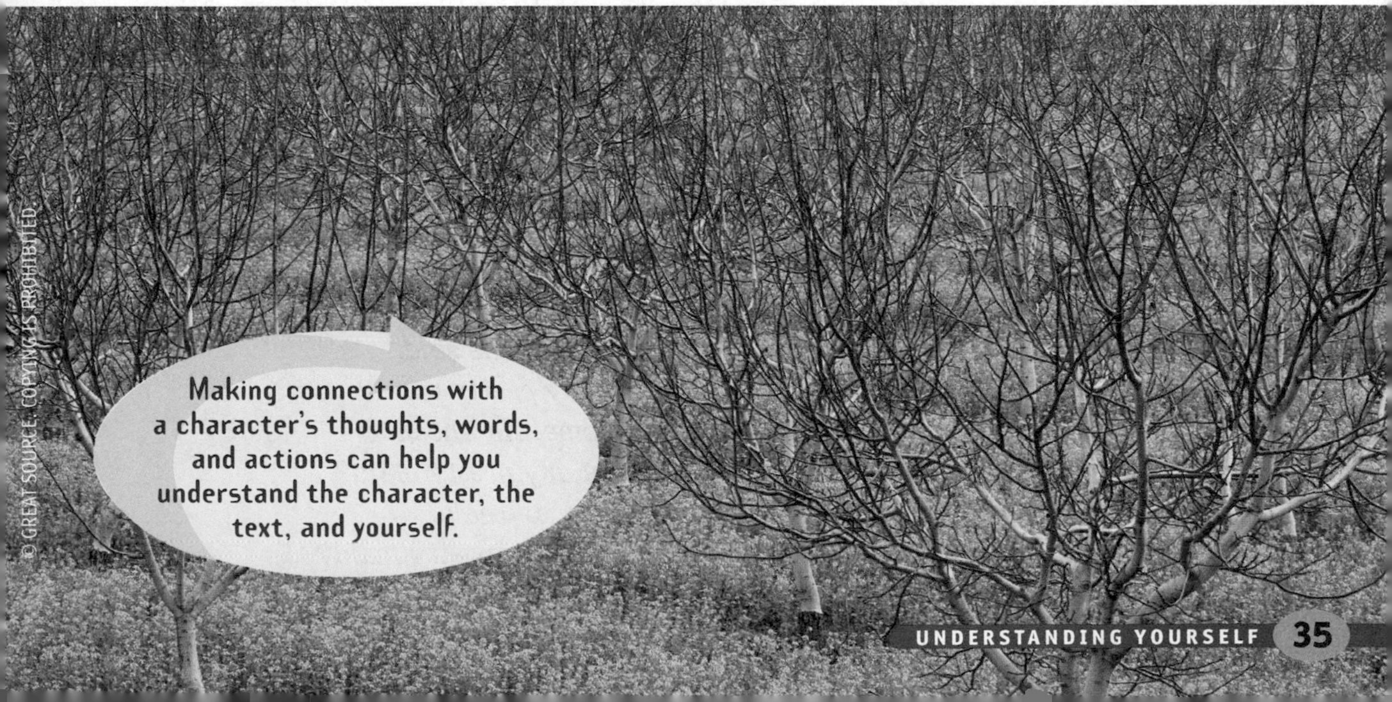

Making connections with a character's thoughts, words, and actions can help you understand the character, the text, and yourself.

Solving problems is a common theme in stories, books, and articles. People and characters often solve their problems by making connections in their own lives.

In the late 1700s, Edward Jenner was a country doctor in England. He was curious about a disease called smallpox. Almost everyone who was exposed to the disease got sick—except for the milkmaids. What was so special about them?

As you read this nonfiction passage, notice the connections Edward Jenner makes as he tries to understand the disease. Underline the text that shows his connections. Write about the connections in your **Response Notes**.

Response Notes

from Dr. Jenner and the Speckled Monster by Albert Marrin

The idea had first crossed [Jenner's] mind before 1770, during his stay with Mr. Ludlow. Like all country surgeons, Mr. Ludlow had milkmaids for patients, young women who made their living by milking dairy cows. While calling at a farm one day, Jenner had struck up a conversation with a pretty milkmaid. After a while the subject of smallpox came up. Had she ever been inoculated, he asked. No, she replied. Still, she did not fear the disease, since "I cannot take [get] smallpox, for I have had cowpox."

During visits to other farms, Jenner heard milkmaids sing as they went about their work:

Where are you going, my pretty maid?
I'm going a-milking, sir, she said.
May I go with you, my pretty maid?
You're kindly welcome, sir, she said.
What is your father, my pretty maid?
My father's a farmer, she said.
What is your fortune, my pretty maid?

Milkmaids' faces were their fortunes, as the song said, because they had clear, smooth skin unmarked by smallpox scars, and could find husbands anytime they wished to marry. Although smallpox might tear through the rest of the community, it seemed to pass them by. And that, they said, was because they had already had "the cowpox."

Cowpox was a mild disease of cattle, found only in the British Isles and western Europe. Most likely, Jenner saw it on the milking cow his brother owned. (Many people, not just farmers, kept cows.) The infection appeared on an infected cow's udder and teats as red, swollen patches with bluish pustules at the center. The animal became restless and feverish, giving less milk. After a week or so, the symptoms passed and the cow recovered. Yet Jenner had never heard of a connection between cowpox and smallpox until the milkmaids mentioned it to him. When he told Mr. Ludlow of their claim, the surgeon called it an ignorant superstition. Later, John Hunter said the same thing. By then, in any case, other ideas filled Jenner's mind. He let the matter drop, burying himself in his studies.

Eight years later, however, as the smallpox epidemic of 1778 struck Berkeley and the surrounding countryside, Jenner recalled the milkmaid's words. The surgeon began to ask about cowpox during his rounds. Sure enough, the milkmaids he spoke to who had gotten cowpox remained free of smallpox, although they lived near people who were coming down with the dread disease. Farmers also repeated the folk saying: "If you want to marry a woman who will never be scarred by the pox, marry a milkmaid."

Did cowpox really prevent smallpox? Jenner wondered. If so, how? Was getting cowpox safer than having an inoculation? That could be an exciting discovery. But was it true? Mr. Hunter had taught him how to find out. Jenner must look carefully and gather his facts. Then, he must *try the experiment.* ❖

✻ **What was the main connection Edward Jenner noticed about smallpox?**

....

....

....

....

....

✻ **What is your explanation for why the milkmaids didn't get infected with smallpox?**

....

....

....

....

....

Notice how characters and people make connections in their own lives. That will help you better understand the text.

7 LESSON

Books can remind you of other books, movies, or TV shows. Sometimes an author purposely includes specific words or phrases from other books, movies, or TV shows, hoping that you'll recognize them. These connections will help you better understand the text.

As you read *Love That Dog* and "The Pasture," notice any connections you make with other poems or stories. Also, look for clues that show how these two poems connect with each other. Write what you notice in the **Response Notes**.

from Love That Dog by Sharon Creech

November 9
I don't have any pets
so I can't write about one
and especially
I can't write
a POEM
about one.

November 15
Yes, I used to have a pet.
I don't want to write
   about it.

You're going to ask me
Why not?
Right?

November 22
Pretend I still have
   that pet?

Can't I make up a pet—
a different one?
Like a tiger?
Or a hamster?
A goldfish?
Turtle?
Snail?
Worm?
Flea? ▶

Response Notes

Response Notes

November 29
I liked those
small poems
we read today.

When they're small
like that
you can read
a whole bunch
in a short time
and then in your head
are all the pictures
of all the small things
from all the small poems.

I liked how the kitten leaped
in the cat poem
and how you could see
the long head of the horse
in the horse poem
and especially I liked the dog
in the dog poem
because that's just how
my yellow dog
used to lie down,
with his tongue all limp
and his chin
between
his paws
and how he'd sometimes
chomp at a fly
and then sleep
in his loose skin,
just like that poet,
Miss Valerie Worth,
says,
in her small
dog poem.

December 4
Why do you want
to type up what I wrote
about reading
the small poems?

It's not a poem.
Is it?

I guess you can
put it on the board
if you want to
but don't put
my name
on it
in case
other people
think
it's not a poem.

December 13
I guess it does
look like a poem
when you see it
typed up
like that.

But I think maybe
it would look better
if there was more space
between the lines.
Like how I wrote it
the first time.

And I liked the picture
of the yellow dog
you put beside it.

But that's not how
my yellow dog
looked.

January 10
I really really really
did NOT get
the pasture poem
you read today.

I mean:
somebody's going out
to the pasture
to clean the spring
and to get

the little tottery calf
while he's out there
and he isn't going
to be gone long
and he wants YOU
(who is YOU?)
to come too.

I mean REALLY.

And you said that
Mr. Robert Frost
who wrote
about the pasture
was also the one
who wrote about
those snowy woods
and the miles to go
before he sleeps—
well!

I think Mr. Robert Frost
has a little
too
much
time
on his
hands.

January 17
Remember the wheel-
  barrow poem
you read
the first week
of school?

Maybe the wheelbarrow
poet
was just
making a picture
with words
and
someone else—
like maybe his teacher—
typed it up

and then people thought
it was a poem
because
it looked like one
typed up like that.

And maybe
that's the same thing
that happened with
Mr. Robert Frost.
Maybe he was just
making pictures with
  words
about the snowy woods
and the pasture—
and his teacher
typed them up
and they *looked* like poems
so people thought
they were poems.

Like how you did
with the blue-car things
and reading-the-small-
poems thing.
On the board
typed up
they look like
poems
and the other kids
are looking at them
and they think
they really are
poems
and they
are all saying
Who wrote that? ✢

The Pasture by Robert Frost

I'm going out to clean the pasture spring;
I'll only stop to rake the leaves away
(And wait to watch the water clear, I may):
I shan't be gone long. — You come too.

I'm going out to fetch the little calf
That's standing by the mother. It's so young,
It totters when she licks it with her tongue.
I shan't be gone long. — You come too. ❖

✳ Find and underline the lines in *Love That Dog* that connect with "The Pasture." How do the author's words help you connect the two poems?

✳ In *Love That Dog*, how do the narrator's feelings about poetry change?

Making connections across texts can help you understand the author's meaning.

When a poem tells a story about a character, you can connect to the character's thoughts, feelings, words, and actions. Making connections to the character and the poem will help you understand them.

As you read "Jake's Plea," try to recall a time when you made a plea for something. What does it feel like to make a plea? Why does someone make a plea? In the **Response Notes**, write connections you make with the poem.

Response Notes

Jake's Plea by Carole Boston Weatherford

The mother tongue has left Jake's lips;
he shrieks in silence at the whip.
His shirt is ragged; broad back scarred.
He labors long; his life is hard.

He floods the fields where rice will grow,
yet Master reaps the grain Jake sows.
At harvesttime from dawn to dusk,
he separates the grain from husk.

Running barefoot through the dirt
not knowing they'll be forced to work,
slave children, in the quarter, stay
and, with the master's children, play.

By moonlight, Jake kneels down to pray,
"Don't let my kin be sold away."
This plea, he makes most every night,
then shuts his eyes and dreams of flight. ❖

✳ List two things Jake says, does, thinks, or feels. Then write the connections you make.

Jake's words, thoughts, feelings, or actions	What connections do you make?

✳ Jake speaks one line in the poem. What is he talking about?

....

....

....

....

✳ What is Jake's dream? Explain.

....

....

....

....

....

✳ **What have you learned about making connections?**

....

....

....

....

....

✳ **Why do you think making connections helps you better understand what you're reading?**

....

....

....

....

Making connections with what happens in a poem helps you understand the poem and yourself.

Asking Questions

When you walk out of a movie, you probably ask yourself a lot of questions. *What happened at the end? Why did the main character say that?*

You can also ask questions about what you read. **Asking questions** before you read helps you gather background knowledge and set a purpose. Asking questions as you read helps you better understand and engage in the topic. Asking questions after you read helps you connect ideas and recall details.

In this unit, you will practice asking questions about what you read. The selections are all about **change makers**—people whose personal missions or goals changed not only their lives but also the lives of others.

In this lesson, you will read a **biographical sketch** about the famous musician B.B. King. He plays the blues, a form of music that started in the American South about a hundred years ago. It combines parts of African music with parts of American music. Even though blues singers often sing about unhappy times, many people feel great joy from the music.

What do you want to find out about B.B. King? **Asking questions** sets a purpose for reading. As you read, your mind searches for the answers.

Before you read, write your questions in the **Response Notes.** Use the picture and quotation to spark ideas. As you read, add any new questions and underline any answers you find.

B.B. King by Julius Lester

Words aren't my friends. Music is. Sounds, notes, rhythms. I talk through music. My aim is to express the longing in my soul and the joy in my heart. If I do that, I feel fulfilled.

—*B.B. King*

He was born Riley B. King, but the "B" didn't stand for anything. His parents divorced when he was four or five and his mother moved to a plantation outside Kilmichael, Mississippi, where he lived with her and his grandmother. He was milking twenty cows a day by age six.

B.B.'s mother and grandmother died before he was eleven. He could have lived with relatives on the plantation, but B.B. said that "from ages ten until thirteen I lived alone." His relatives probably saw to it that he was fed every day, but B.B. said he "didn't want to live with anyone except the memory of my mother and her mother."

He was thirteen when his father appeared one day and said, "You're gonna live with me now." B.B. was both excited and scared to go live with his father in the town of Lexington, Mississippi. But after six months B.B. was so unhappy, he left without telling his father and went

Response Notes

What does "B.B." stand for?

How did he learn to play?

How did he become famous?

back to the plantation. It took him two days to get there on his bicycle. But someone was living in what had been his cabin, and his relatives had moved to a plantation outside Indianola, Mississippi, so he went there.

Music was always part of B.B.'s life. He once said that the music he heard in church "got all over my body and made me wanna jump." The preacher of his church, Archie Fair, was a relative who gave B.B. his first guitar lessons, telling him the guitar was "another way to express God's love."

B.B. also listened to the records of Blind Lemon Jefferson, whom B.B. liked because he "put so much feeling into his words until I believed everything he sang. [He] was strong and direct and bone-close to my home." B.B. still listens to Blind Lemon's music every day.

He joined a group called the "Famous St. John Gospel Singers," but he also liked going to a club in Indianola to listen to jazz and blues. Too young to go inside, B.B. stood in the alley and looked through the slats of the building. The Count Basie Band, Charlie Parker, and bluesmen Sonny Boy Williamson and Robert Junior Lockwood, Robert Johnson's stepson, were some of the great musicians he heard there. The shows ended late at night and B.B. had to walk eight miles back to the plantation. He said he didn't mind because "I'd still hear those blues; under the glow of a white Mississippi moon, I'd sing the blues out loud, singing to the birds or the squirrels or to God above, singing because my heart was happy."

✳ **What new questions do you have?**

He began singing on street corners in Indianola and quickly learned that people put more money in his hat when he sang the blues than when he sang gospel. B.B. dropped out of school in the tenth grade. "The longer I live, the more I see how I shortchanged myself. I hate that I never went to college. I feel like I'm missing a component—a way of understanding the world—that only more schooling could have provided," he has lamented.

At age twenty, B.B. went to Memphis, Tennessee, and to the street there that is famous for the blues, Beale Street. When B.B. talked a radio station into giving him a daily ten-minute show, the station decided to call him Beale Street Blues Boy. He started getting mail addressed to "Blues Boy" and was soon known simply as "B.B."

In 1952, he had his first hit record, "Three O'Clock Blues," and has been recording and performing ever since. He has received more honorary degrees from colleges and universities than any other blues singer, as well as numerous music awards. These include seventeen Grammy nominations and seven Grammys, and election to the Blues Foundation Hall of Fame in 1980 and the Rock and Roll Hall of Fame in 1987, with Muddy Waters and Aretha Franklin. He won an MTV video award for a video he did with Bono and U2. He was invited to the White House by presidents Bush and Clinton, played for Queen Elizabeth and Prince Philip of England, and has a star on the Hollywood Walk of Fame.

B.B. has a home in Las Vegas, Nevada, where he keeps a collection of a million records, CDs, videotapes, and books. Even though he dropped out of school in the tenth grade, he loves to read. A funny thing about B.B., though, is that because his grandmother told him scary stories when he was a boy, he's still afraid of the dark and sleeps with a night-light on.

B.B. is the master of playing on one string of his guitar. He plays in short, piercing phrases that make you feel like something is biting at your soul. Lucille, which is what he calls his guitar, is like another voice, singing in pure music what there are no words for. When he plays, B.B. closes his eyes and scrunches up his face like he's in pain. But that's because his feelings are going straight from his heart into his fingers. ❖

✳ List three facts you learned about B.B. King.

....

....

....

....

✳ How did B.B. King get his name?

....

....

....

....

✳ If you could choose a nickname for yourself, what would it be? Why?

....

....

....

....

....

Look at pictures, quotations, captions, and headings to spark questions about what you think you will learn.

When you read, you can **question the author.**
You might ask:

- What does the author want me to understand from the title?

- What big ideas does the author want me to understand from the details?

Questioning the author and looking for answers will help you more fully understand your reading.

Folk music tells about the lives of ordinary people. One of the best-loved American folk singers was Woody Guthrie. His songs changed American music.

During the Great Depression of the 1930s, Woody traveled from state to state. He spent time with workers of all kinds—farmers, sailors, cowboys, factory workers, and others. He listened to their stories and learned their songs.

Before you read this biographical sketch, think about the title of the passage. What does it mean? As you read, underline details that show big ideas. In the **Response Notes**, write the big ideas.

Response Notes

from This Land Was Made for You and Me by Elizabeth Partridge

Woody said the best songs came to him when he was walking down a road. He always had fifteen or twenty songs running around in his mind, just waiting to be put together. Sometimes he knew the words, but not the melody. Usually he'd borrow a tune that was already well known—the simpler the better. As he walked along, he tried to catch a good, easy song that people could sing the first time they heard it, remember, and sing again later.

Woody sang his songs the old-fashioned way, his voice droning and nasal, the words sharp and clear. Promoters and club owners wanted him to follow their tightly written scripts and sing the melodious, popular songs that were on the radio. Whenever they came at him with their hands full of cash, Woody ran the other way. "I had rather sound like the cab drivers cursing at one another, like the longshoremen yelling, like the cowhands whooping and like the lone wolf barking, than to sound like a slick, smooth tongued, oily lipped, show person."

Just after New Year's Day in 1940, Woody set off on one of his unannounced road trips. He left his wife and three kids in a shack in Texas and headed for New York City. It was a long, cold trip in the dead of winter, and every time he stopped in a diner he heard Irving Berlin's lush, sentimental song, "God Bless America," on the jukebox. It was exactly the kind of song Woody couldn't stand, romanticizing America, telling people not to worry, that God would take care of everything.

Woody thought there was plenty to worry about. The Great Depression, which had begun in 1929, was grinding on. For years, desperate, hungry people had been tramping the roads and riding the rails, looking for work or handouts. In Europe another world war was raging, threatening to pull America into the bloody conflict.

Response Notes

Bits of tunes and snatches of words swirled in Woody's mind, and a few weeks later in a cheap, fleabag hotel in New York City, his own song about America came together. Using an old Baptist tune for the melody, Woody wrote "This Land Is Your Land." His song caught the bittersweet contrasts of America: the beauty of our country, and the desperate strength of people making do in impossibly difficult times. Across the bottom of the sheet Woody wrote in his neat script, "All you can write is what you see," and put the song away.

Writing about what he saw—and felt, and heard about, and read about—gave Woody plenty of material. During his lifetime he wrote down more than three thousand songs, taking stories from everywhere: the front page of the newspaper; union meetings and busted-up strikes; and the sights and sounds of America as he walked "that ribbon of highway." ❖

✳ **Reread the title. What ideas do you think the author wants you to think about?**

✳ **Find the quotation from Woody Guthrie on page 53 that begins, "I had rather sound like the cab drivers . . ." Read the whole quotation. Why did the author include this? What does it tell you about Woody Guthrie?**

✳ What were Woody Guthrie's values and beliefs?
What are yours? Fill in the chart. Is there any overlap
between your beliefs and Woody Guthrie's beliefs?

Woody Guthrie's values and beliefs	Your values and beliefs

Questioning the author
helps you understand
the author's main ideas.

Each person has a **point of view**, or way of looking at things. Sometimes an author will describe an event through more than one point of view. If the point of view changes, the way the reader sees the event can change, too.

This nonfiction passage is about Marian Anderson, a great singer who grew up in the 1920s and 1930s—a time of segregation in the South. In 1939, a group of people refused to let Marian sing in Constitution Hall in Washington, D.C., because of her race. Many people, including President and Mrs. Roosevelt, were unhappy about that. As a result, members of the U.S. government organized another concert for her. Seventy-five thousand people came to hear Marian Anderson at the Lincoln Memorial.

As you read about the concert, underline the three different points of view the author includes. In the **Response Notes**, write questions about the points of view.

Response Notes

from The Voice That Challenged a Nation by Russell Freedman

Anderson rose from her seat. She wore a mink coat and a bright orange-and-yellow scarf about her neck, and she was bareheaded. Drawing her coat closely around her shoulders against the wind, she moved toward the microphones. "She looked regal and dignified as she came forward with slow steps," Vehanen [Anderson's pianist] remembered. "When she came to the place where the steps began to descend, she stopped for a moment as she gazed over the enormous gathering of people. Her breath seemed to leave her for that fleeting moment, but I think that those who were privileged to see her at that time were much more moved than she was."

Anderson faced the now hushed and expectant crowd that stretched across the Mall from the base of the Lincoln Memorial all the way to the Washington Monument.

Directly behind her, the great Lincoln Memorial was filled with shadow in the late-afternoon light. And the statue of Lincoln looked almost ready to speak.

"There seemed to be people as far as the eye could see," Anderson recalled. "I had a feeling that a great wave of good will poured out from these people, almost engulfing me. And when I stood up to sing . . . I felt for a moment as though I were choking. For a desperate second I thought that the words, well as I knew them, would not come. I sang, I don't know how."

"My feelings were so deep that I have never forgotten it, and I don't think until I leave this earth I will ever forget it," recalled opera and theater performer Todd Duncan. "Number one, I never have been so proud to be an American. Number two, I never have been so proud to be an American Negro. And number three, I never felt such pride [as] in seeing this Negro woman stand up there with this great regal dignity and sing.

"In back of me were the Tidal Basin and Washington Monument. Under my feet was the grass. To the side of me the walls were beautiful trees. The ceiling was the sky. And in front of me were those wonderful majestic stairs going up to the Lincoln Memorial. And there stood Miss Anderson. . . . The highlight of that day were the first words that she sang."

Closing her eyes, Marian Anderson began to sing, and her thrilling contralto voice carried across the Mall, touching every person who had come to hear her. Her opening number was "America," and the words "sweet land of liberty" poured from her almost as a prayer:

My country, 'tis of thee,
Sweet land of liberty,
To thee we sing;
Land where my fathers died,
Land of the Pilgrims' pride,
From every mountain-side
Let Freedom ring!

She did not use the "I" as she sang. In her rendition "Of thee I sing" was replaced by "*To* thee *we* sing." ❖

✳ Look back at the quotations from Kosti Vehanen, Marian Anderson, and Todd Duncan. What do their words show you about this moment in history?

Point of view of . . .	What do you learn from their words?
Kosti Vehanen	
Marian Anderson	
Todd Duncan	

✳ List three traits that Marian Anderson probably had that helped her perform at the Lincoln Memorial.

....

....

....

....

✳ Think about B.B. King, Woody Guthrie, and Marian Anderson. What connections can you make between music and creating change in the world?

....

....

....

....

....

....

Questioning the author about points of view helps you understand a text from different angles.

When you read factual information, look for a **main idea**. A main idea is a central point that the author makes. It is always supported by details. Sometimes an author directly states the main idea. Other times you have to figure it out.

Question the author to find and understand the main ideas. As you read, ask:

- What does the author want me to understand about the details in this passage?

Read the following informational passage. In the **Response Notes,** write what you think the author wants you to understand. Underline important points the author makes.

Response Notes

from Mistakes That Worked
by Charlotte Jones

World War I lasted more than four years—from 1914 to 1918. During that time, approximately 8.5 million people were killed and 21 million were wounded.

Near the end of World War I, a doctor was walking outside a German military hospital with a soldier who had been blinded in battle. The doctor's dog joined the walk and when the doctor was called into one of the buildings, the blind soldier was left alone with the dog.

Soon the doctor returned, but the blind man and the dog were missing. When he found them, he discovered the dog had led the blind patient across the hospital grounds.

The doctor was amazed at what his untrained pet dog had done and decided to see how well a trained working breed of dog could lead a blind person. The results were great and the German government soon expanded the dog guide program.

An American woman named Dorothy Eustis visited Potsdam, Germany, to learn about the dog guide program. Through an article she wrote for *The Saturday Evening*

Post, she brought the program to public attention in the United States. The first American dog guide school, The Seeing Eye, Inc., was established in 1929. Today ten major organizations train dogs and instruct blind people in their use.

The most popular breeds are German shepherds, golden retrievers, and Labrador retrievers. They must learn hand gestures and simple commands in order to lead the blind person across streets and around people, obstacles, holes, and low-hanging awnings or tree limbs.

The dog must also learn to exercise good judgment. If the blind person gives a "forward" command but the dog sees danger, the dog must know when to disobey. This is called "intelligent disobedience."

Dogs guiding blind masters is not new. Wall paintings, ancient scrolls, and legends tell of dogs leading blind men since 100 B.C. But until the German soldier was led by the doctor's untrained dog and the first training program was initiated, the incidents were scattered and the dogs were not always efficient.

In the case of dog guides, the old saying is true: A dog really is a man's—or a woman's—best friend. ❖

✳ Use the idea web to jot down a few of the points the author makes about guide dog programs.

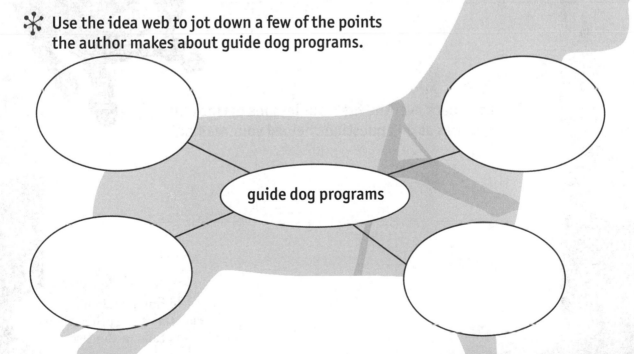

guide dog programs

✱ Decide what the author's most important point is. Try writing some important details first. Then think about the big idea that grows out of the details.

Important/supporting details:

1. ....
....

2. ....
....

3. ....
....

Main idea:

✱ Look back over the first four lessons of this unit. How has asking questions helped your reading?

....

....

....

....

To find a main idea, question the author about details in the text.

Imagine if you had to work fourteen hours a day, six days a week in a hot, dark factory. Child labor of this sort is against the law in the United States. But it still exists in other parts of the world. Iqbal Masih, a boy from Pakistan, was forced to work like that from the age of four.

As you read this informational piece about Iqbal, notice the questions that arise in your mind. Write them in the **Response Notes.** Asking questions about an unfamiliar topic will help you better understand it.

When you finish the selection, think about the questions you asked. Asking questions after you read will strengthen your ability to recall details and make lasting connections.

from Stolen Dreams by David L. Parker

Response Notes

Each morning, six days a week, more than half a million children between the ages of four and fourteen rise before dawn and make their way along dark country roads leading to Pakistan's carpet factories. Most of these children must be at work by 6:00 A.M. If they are late, they may be punished—hit with a wooden cane, or worse, hung upside down, their ankles tightly bound with rope. The carpet weavers work 14 hours a day, with only a 30-minute break for lunch.

Iqbal Masih was one of these workers. He started working in a carpet factory when he was just four years old. His parents were poor farmers living near Lahore, the largest city in Pakistan. Because they did not have enough money to feed their children or buy them clothes, Iqbal's parents made a very difficult choice. In exchange for a small sum of money, about $16, they agreed to send their son to work in a nearby carpet factory until he had earned enough money to pay back the loan. Iqbal was told he would be paid three cents a day for his work.

A man named Arshad owned the factory. Inside, the only light came from two bare light bulbs that hung in the middle of the room like dragon's eyes. Only a few flecks of paint dotted the walls. The carpet looms looked as though they were a hundred years old. Two strong wooden beams ran across the top and bottom of each loom's frame, which had been created by driving four large stakes into the ground.

In front of each loom sat a small child on a piece of wood scaffolding. The young weaver would tie short lengths of brightly colored thread to a warp of heavier white threads. To make just one carpet, workers had to tie more than a million small knots into a colorful rhythm of circles, squares, and other intricate designs. In the United States, hand-knotted carpets such as these sell for more than $2,000 each.

The scaffold bench could be moved up or down as the child worked on the rug, so the rug did not have to be moved. Except for a rare and forbidden whisper, the children never spoke to one another. "If I let them talk, I know they will start making mistakes," Iqbal's boss said. "And when they make mistakes, I lose money."

If the children complained about how they were treated, they were beaten. Over the years, Iqbal received many cuts and bruises from Arshad's punishments. And Iqbal found out what would happen if he talked back or tried to force Arshad to stop treating the workers so badly.

✳ What questions do you have about Iqbal so far?

....

....

....

....

....

One night, when Iqbal was 10 years old, Arshad pulled him out of bed at 3:00 A.M. and ordered him to repair some carpets. Iqbal went to the local police to complain. He told them that his boss had beat him up and showed them the bruises on his arms. One of the police officers glared at Iqbal. He told him he had no right to complain—he'd better stick to his work and do what he was told. The officer grabbed Iqbal by his sore arm and led him back to the factory. "If he tries this again, chain him to his loom," the officer told Arshad.

Arshad did chain Iqbal to his loom. Even when Iqbal hurt so much he could hardly move, he fought back. He believed that what Arshad was doing was wrong.

At 10 years old, Iqbal was just under 4 feet tall, the normal size of a child who is two or three years younger. He weighed less than 60 pounds. From years of sitting hunched in front of the loom, his spine curved like that of an old man. When Iqbal walked, his feet shuffled slowly, as though he were wearing slippers that were too big.

Arshad told Iqbal that the harder he worked, the faster the loan made to his parents would be paid off. But no matter what Iqbal did, the loan just got bigger and bigger. Iqbal's father left home, and his mother was forced to borrow more money from Arshad. By the time Iqbal was 11 years old, his loan had increased to $419—more than 25 times the original amount. When Iqbal heard this, he knew he would be trapped forever unless he found a way to escape.

✳ What new questions do you have about Iqbal?

....

....

✳ What is one memorable fact you've read so far?

....

....

Response Notes

In the summer of 1992, Iqbal heard about a meeting to be held in a nearby town. A man named Essan Ulla Khan was going to speak about a new law forbidding carpet factories to employ children. Iqbal decided he must go to this meeting.

On the day of the meeting, Iqbal had worked almost 16 hours. In Arshad's factory there were no fans and no open windows. In the summer, the heat climbed to 120 degrees Fahrenheit. When Iqbal finally made it to the meeting, he was exhausted and very hot. He managed to push his way through the crowd to the front. He sat on the floor below the platform where Khan was speaking.

Khan talked about an organization called the Bonded Labor Liberation Front (BLLF). Its goal was to free Pakistan's bonded laborers. Like Iqbal, they were treated as slaves. The companies they worked for owned them just as they owned property or buildings. The workers were not free to leave their jobs. Khan said that thousands of children worked in bondage in Pakistan's textile and brick factories, tanneries, and steelworks. Under the new law, bonded laborers did not have to work if they did not want to.

When Khan finished speaking, several people jumped up to ask questions. Finally Khan noticed Iqbal's small raised hand and told the audience to let the boy speak. After a pause, Iqbal asked quietly, "How can I stop working and go to school?" Khan explained that Iqbal had new rights under the law. He could show Arshad some legal papers and Arshad would have to let Iqbal go. Khan also told Iqbal about the schools that the BLLF sponsored for children who had been bonded laborers.

The next morning, when Iqbal returned to the carpet factory, he took the legal papers with him. He told Arshad he would no longer work, nor would he pay his debt, because bonded labor was illegal. Arshad's face grew red with anger. He cursed at Iqbal and beat him. But Iqbal escaped and ran out of the factory.

Two days later, Arshad came to Iqbal's home, demanding that Iqbal return to the factory or pay the money he said the family owed. Iqbal stood his ground. He knew he could count on his new friend for help.

Khan did help Iqbal get away from the factory. He threatened to have Arshad arrested if he protested. Khan greatly admired Iqbal's courage and perseverance. He found Iqbal a place in a BLLF primary school in Lahore. ❖

✳ **What are three surprising or memorable facts from this selection?**

1. ....

....

....

2. ....

....

....

3. ....

....

....

✳ Look back at the selection and your Response Notes. What are two big ideas the author wants you to understand?

....

....

....

....

✳ What connections can you make with Iqbal's story? Fill in the chart with your thoughts.

How does Iqbal's story connect with . . .	Your thoughts
The Voice That Challenged a Nation?	
another book, TV show, or movie you've seen? List the title.	
a current or historical situation?	

✳ Plan and write a speech that Iqbal might have given to your class.

....

....

....

....

....

....

....

....

....

....

....

....

Asking questions after reading
helps you recall details
and make connections.

The selection below is also about Iqbal, but it's from a fiction book based on Iqbal's true story. Maria, the letter writer, had been working with Iqbal to help free other child workers.

As you read the passage, notice the similarities and differences in how two different authors treat the same topic. Think about these questions:

- How is fiction different from nonfiction?

- How is *Iqbal* similar to or different from *Stolen Dreams*?

As you read, underline new information you learn about Iqbal. In the **Response Notes**, write your questions.

Response Notes

from **Iqbal** by Francesco D'Adamo
and translated by Ann Leonori

Dear Fatima, my friend, beloved sister,

How I wish you were near me these days, so I could talk to you and cry with your arms around me. Do you remember how many times I've done so in the past? And you were always able to find the best way to console me and to protect me. If you could only do it once more! If we could only share our common grief! If only I could be the one to find the right words!

I know I haven't written for a long time. Maybe you thought I had forgotten you, that my affection had vanished like the mist on morning fields. My silence was because I didn't want to be the one to break the news to you. Even now my hand trembles and my tears fall. Forgive my cowardice, Fatima. I know you mustn't learn from others—who knows what they might say? I'll tell you.

At Easter, the Christian festival, Iqbal went home to his village. He went there to visit his family and celebrate. He was supposed to spend a month with his parents, and then return to us, to continue his work. He said that he had made a promise in front of all those people in America, and that he meant to keep it.

You know what he was like.

They say that the village welcomed him joyfully, like a hero. Everyone knew what he had done and they admired and respected him. Everybody in the village visited his home, brought him presents, and asked if it was true that he had been in a plane.

They say that after two days he was tired of all this attention and began avoiding people. He preferred to get up at dawn and go out into the fields with his father instead. In the afternoons, he rode an old bicycle with his two younger cousins, or together they flew kites. He was happy and serene and full of plans for the future.

They say that Easter Sunday was a lovely day, full of sunshine and light. Iqbal went to his church and then went around to visit relatives. There was a big feast, with singing and dancing, and there was even meat to eat, and all kinds of sweets, and Iqbal ate enough **laddu** to cause a stomachache. Then, while the adults were talking among themselves, the children scattered off to play, and their voices could be heard in the distance.

They say that around three that afternoon—when the sun was beginning to go down—a car appeared just where the road turns in toward the village, raising a cloud of dust. Nobody recognized it. It was a big black car, covered with mud. It looked as though it was driving by itself, and it whipped up the gravel with its enormous wheels as it passed.

Some people say that at that precise moment a sudden thunderstorm broke, and raindrops the size of large coins hit the ground and the thunder shook the roofs of the houses. Others say that the thunderstorm broke later, toward evening.

The black car drove slowly through the village and then turned into a narrow lane that leads down to the rice paddies. The pouring rain and the water in the rice paddies merged as one.

They say that Iqbal was riding up the lane, standing so that he could pedal better, with his wet hair in his eyes and his T-shirt flapping in the wind.

Nobody knows what happened, Fatima, my sister. A man has murmured that through the curtain of falling rain he saw Iqbal pass close to the car. The window came down a little, and there were three, four, maybe five flashes. Before anyone could get the men together and run to help, the car had disappeared. Iqbal's body was there, fallen in the lane, and the water under him was stained red, but even the red water disappeared soon. The rain washed it away. This is what they have told me.

But listen, Fatima. I know it's not true.

At first I thought I had become mute again. I had closed up inside. I kept saying to myself, "It's not true, you know what people are like, how they imagine things, how rumors persist." Everyone else was convinced the news was true, even Eshan Khan and his wife. I was the only one who didn't believe it.

Then, one afternoon two weeks ago, there was a knock on the garden door. It was a boy, dirty and with bruises from chains around his ankles. He told us he had been working in a carpet factory, that he had run away and come to us so that we would help arrest his master and free the other children.

And then, do you want to know what he said?

"I'm not afraid."

I looked at him carefully, Fatima. It was Iqbal. I swear, he was identical! The same voice, the same eyes.

Three days later another boy appeared. And then at the market a boy rebelled against his master, one of the richest merchants.

They were Iqbal, too.

Try not to be sad, Fatima. He changed our lives and will be with us forever. I told Eshan Khan that I'll be the one to study and go to university. I'll be a lawyer, and I'll fight to free all the slaves in Pakistan and all over the world. And for the first time in my life, I'm not afraid either.

My sister, I don't know where you're going, or how I'll be able to communicate with you, or even if we'll meet again. I just beg of you, don't forget. Tell somebody our story. Tell everybody our story. So that the memory will not be lost.

That's the only way to keep Iqbal at our sides forever. Your sister,
Maria. ❖

❋ What did you learn in this selection that wasn't in *Stolen Dreams*?

....

....

....

❋ Think about how *Iqbal* and *Stolen Dreams* are similar and different. Write your thoughts in the Venn diagram.

Iqbal   **Stolen Dreams**

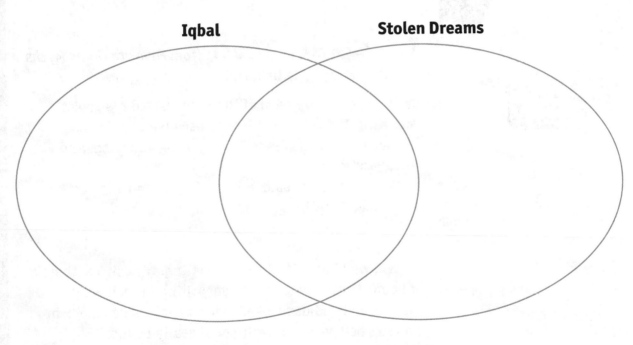

❋ Why might this author have chosen to write a fiction piece rather than an informational piece about Iqbal?

....

....

....

Comparing two texts on a similar topic will help you better understand both texts.

Suppose you go to a party where you don't know anyone. What would you do? You'd probably find a friendly person and start a conversation. But what would you say? You don't know the person at all. Chances are you'd introduce yourself and ask a question.

When you "meet" characters for the first time, you can ask them questions, too. Of course, they can't answer you, but your questions will help you find the answers.

As you read this famous Greek myth, write questions in the **Response Notes** that help you "get to know" King Midas. Underline the sentences that tell you about his personality.

Response Notes

The Golden Touch from *Favorite Greek Myths*
retold by Mary Pope Osborne

Bacchus, the merry god of the vine, raised his goblet. "To you, King Midas," he said, "and because you have been so hospitable to me—ask for anything you wish, and I will grant it to you."

"What an idea!" said Midas. "Anything I wish?"

"Indeed, anything," said Bacchus.

"Anything?"

"Yes! Yes!"

"Ah, well," said the king, chuckling. "Of course, there's only one thing: I wish that everything I touch would turn to gold!" Midas looked sideways at Bacchus, for he couldn't believe such a gift could really be his.

"My friend, you already have all the gold you could possibly want," said Bacchus, looking disappointed.

"Oh, no! I don't!" said Midas. "One never has enough gold!"

"Well, if that's what you wish for, I suppose I will have to grant it," said Bacchus.

Bacchus soon took his leave. As Midas waved good-bye to him, his hand brushed an oak twig hanging from a tree—and the twig turned to gold!

The king screamed with joy, then shouted after Bacchus, "My wish has come true! Thank you! Thank you!"

The god turned and waved, then disappeared down the road. ❖

✳ How do you think King Midas would answer these questions? Write your thoughts. Then add your own question.

Questions for King Midas	What you think King Midas would say
Why do you want everything you touch to turn to gold?	
What do you mean by "one never has enough gold"?	

✳ Now that you've questioned King Midas, what have you learned about him?

....

....

....

....

....

....

Ask questions about story characters to better understand their actions.

When you read fiction, question the author for a **theme**. A theme is a story's central idea, or a message from the author. As you read, ask yourself: What does the author want me to think or understand from the story? Do any messages jump out at me?

Finish reading "The Golden Touch." Think about the theme or message from the author. Underline sentences or phrases that give clues to a theme. Write thoughts about possible themes in the **Response Notes**.

Response Notes

The Golden Touch
retold by Mary Pope Osborne

Midas looked around excitedly. He leaned over and picked a stone up from the ground—and the stone turned into a golden nugget! He kicked the sand—and the sand turned to golden grains!

King Midas threw back his head and shouted, "I'm the richest man in the world!" Then he rushed about his grounds, touching everything. And everything, *everything* turned to gold: ears of corn in his fields! Apples plucked from trees! The pillars of his mansion!

When the king's servants heard him shouting, they rushed to see what was happening. They found their king dancing wildly on his lawn, turning the grass to glittering blades of gold. Everyone laughed and clapped as Midas washed his hands in his fountain and turned the water to a gleaming spray!

Finally, exhausted but overjoyed, King Midas called for his dinner. His servants placed a huge banquet meal before him on his lawn. "Oh, I'm so hungry!" he said as he speared a piece of meat and brought it to his mouth.

But suddenly King Midas realized his wish may not have been as wonderful as he thought—for the moment he bit down on the meat, it, too, turned to gold.

Midas laughed uneasily, then reached for a piece of bread. But as soon as his hands touched the bread, it also became a hard, golden nugget! Weak with dread, Midas reached for his goblet of water. But alas! His lips touched only hard, cold metal. The water had also turned to gold.

Covering his head and moaning, King Midas realized his great wish was going to kill him. He would starve to death or die of thirst!

"Bacchus!" he cried, throwing his hands toward heaven. "I've been a greedy fool! Take away your gift! Free me from my golden touch! Help me, Bacchus!"

The sobbing king fell off his chair to his knees. He beat his fists against the ground, turning even the little anthills to gold. His servants grieved for him, but none dared go near him, for they feared he might accidently turn them to gold, too!

As everyone wailed with sorrow, Bacchus suddenly appeared on the palace lawn. The merry god stood before the sobbing king for a moment, then said, "Rise, Midas."

Stumbling to his feet, King Midas begged Bacchus to forgive him and to take away the curse of the golden touch.

"You were greedy and foolish, my friend," said Bacchus. "But I will forgive you. Now go and wash yourself in the Pactolus River that runs by Sardis, and you'll be cleansed of this desire to have more gold than anyone else!"

King Midas did as Bacchus said. He washed in the Pactolus, leaving behind streams of gold in the river's sands. Then he returned home and happily ate his dinner. ❖

✳ What are some possible themes, or messages, from the myth? What ideas from the myth support the theme?

Possible theme	Ideas that support the theme
Money isn't everything.	King Midas says, "I've been a greedy fool!"

✳ List three or four ways in which asking questions helps your reading.

1. ....

   ....

2. ....

   ....

3. ....

   ....

4. ....

   ....

   ....

Questioning the author for a theme will help you better understand the central idea of a story.

Determining Importance

You're home with a cold. Your mother returns from the store and says, "I bought some important things for you." She unpacks soup and tissues. She then turns to your brother, who isn't sick, and says, "You have a soccer game tomorrow, and I bought some important things for you, too." Will your brother's important things be the same as yours? Probably not. His important things might be new socks and a water bottle.

When you read, you also make decisions about what is important. You rely on your background knowledge and opinions to help you make choices.

The selections in this unit show different ways people try to **maintain balance** in their lives. As you read, you will become more aware of how your mind **determines the importance** of ideas in a text.

79

DECIDING ABOUT IMPORTANT IDEAS

How do you know which ideas in a text are most important? One of the first things to consider is your **purpose for reading.** Are you reading to find out about a person? Or about an event? Look at the title. Answer this question as your purpose: what happened to the people, houses, and surroundings during the big tsunami of 2004? As you discover the answers, underline the ideas that are most important. Write any questions or thoughts in the **Response Notes.**

Response Notes

Everything and

everyone on

the beach

was swept away.

from Tsunami by Ann Morris and Heidi Larson

At seven o'clock in the morning on December 26, 2004, an earthquake shook the ground on the bottom of the Indian Ocean. The movement on the ocean floor was so strong that it lifted up the millions of tons of ocean water above it. The water mounded up on the ocean's surface, and then the mountain of water began to move. A tsunami was born.

It spread outward in all directions as big flat waves. These waves were very fast, faster than a jet airplane. Within fifteen minutes, the earliest wave hit the coast of Indonesia, sweeping right onto the land and carrying everything on the shoreline along with it, including the people who were living along the beach.

At about the time the earthquake was beginning to rumble under the ocean, two boys in Khao Lak, a small fishing village on the coast of Thailand, were having their breakfast. Twelve-year-old Chaipreak and his younger brother, eight-year-old Chaiya, were making plans for a Sunday of fun on the beautiful beach not far from their home. The boys' parents had lived in the village of Khao Lak for several years and were pleased with the changes that had taken place there in the past decades. Although several of their friends and neighbors still earned their money from fishing, many more worked in the luxurious hotels that had sprung up along the beautiful coastline. Chaipreak and Chaiya's parents were both skilled stone-workers and had helped build helped build several of the beautiful resorts that attracted tourists to their area. The money that their parents earned helped pay for the family's modest home.

The parents had a lot to do that Sunday morning. The boys' mother had to wash a week's worth of family laundry, while their father had to go into the beachside town to help a friend repair his motorcycle. And the boys were going off to the beach to meet their friends. Of course, there was no way the parents could know about what had just happened under the ocean more than 800 miles away, so they happily saw the boys off for their morning of play on the beach. Then they each went out to begin their morning chores.

Chaiya and Chaipreak ran toward the ocean, chasing each other in and out of the trees. Nothing seemed unusual; it was very quiet. <u>There were no animal sounds . . .</u> but they began to hear an unusual roaring sound. And then they saw a huge wave coming right up out of the water and moving straight toward them. The boys were both good climbers, and Chaipreak yelled to Chaiya to get up into a tree! Chaipreak swiftly climbed to the very top of a palm tree, while his brother ran up a cashew tree nearby.

The animals knew about the wave before the people knew.

✳ **What are the most important ideas you've read so far? Talk with a partner about your responses.**

As the boys sat in the tops of the trees, the sound was deafening. When they looked down, they could not believe what they were seeing. The water swept underneath them, carrying everything in its path. Furniture, cars, boats, and even big chunks of houses swirled past them . . . and still the water kept coming!

They were not afraid. The trees felt sturdy beneath them. The water slowed at certain points, but their instincts told them not to come down yet. Just as the water slowed down, it started rushing again—this time back toward the ocean. The boys stayed in their trees for more than an hour, until everything seemed quiet below.

When they came down, their feet sank into the mud, and it was difficult to walk in places as they headed toward their home. What they saw along the way frightened them. They saw injured people still clinging to trees or floating on bits of debris. Cars and even boats were every which way. Familiar sights had changed completely. Houses were not where they once were. When they reached the site where their house used to be, they saw nothing but a field of mud. Their house had been completely swept away along with those of their neighbors.

Their mother was waiting for them near where their house once stood. She was afraid that the tsunami would return. After hugging the boys and seeing that they were all right, she led them to the high ground of the mountains where the tsunami had not reached. That night, they slept on the mountainside. A cousin whose house was partway up the mountain brought them water and food and some clothes to keep them warm. After all they had been through, they were very thankful they had a dry and safe place to spend the night. ❖

Knowing your purpose for reading affects what you think is important in a text.

✳ Use the Response Notes and your purpose for reading to write two more important ideas about what happened during the 2004 tsunami. Then compare and discuss your responses with a classmate's.

Two important ideas	Why they are important

✳ What would be important to do to get your life back to normal after a disaster like this?

....

....

....

....

....

....

Think about your favorite song. Why do you like it? Is it the melody? The lyrics? The guitar solo? There are many levels to a song. A text has different levels, too. You can talk about its ideas, sentences, and words.

The excerpt below is about Abraham Lincoln. Lincoln was president during the Civil War, a time when the balance between the Northern and Southern states was greatly challenged. The Civil War ended on April 9, 1865. Five days later, the president went to see a play. This selection tells about that event.

As you read, underline ideas, sentences, and words that tell about important details. In the **Response Notes**, write your thoughts about why they're important.

Response Notes

from Lincoln: A Photobiography
by Russell Freedman

After dinner, Lincoln and Mary left for Ford's Theatre in the company of a young army major, Henry R. Rathbone, and his fiancée, Clara Harris. Arriving late, they were escorted up a winding stairway to the flag-draped presidential box overlooking the stage. The play had already started, but as Lincoln's party appeared in the box, the orchestra struck up "Hail to the Chief" and the audience rose for a standing ovation. Lincoln smiled and bowed. He took his place in a rocking chair provided for him by the management and put on a pair of gold-rimmed eyeglasses he had mended with a string. Mary sat beside him, with Major Rathbone and Miss Harris to their right.

The play was *Our American Cousin*, a popular comedy starring Laura Keene, who had already given a thousand performances in the leading role. Lincoln settled back and relaxed. He laughed heartily, turning now and then to whisper to his wife. Halfway through the play, he felt a chill and got up to drape his black overcoat across his shoulders.

During the third act, Mary reached over to take Lincoln's hand. She pressed closer to him. Behind them, the door to the presidential box was closed but not locked. Lincoln's bodyguard that evening, John Parker, had slipped away from his post outside the door to go downstairs and watch the play.

The audience had just burst into laughter when the door swung open. A shadowy figure stepped into the box, stretched out his arm, aimed a small derringer pistol at the back of Lincoln's head, and pulled the trigger. Lincoln's arm jerked up. He slumped forward in his chair as Mary reached out to catch him. Then she screamed.

Major Rathbone looked up to see a man standing with a smoking pistol in one hand and a hunting knife in the other. Rathbone lunged at the gunman, who yelled something and slashed Rathbone's arm to the bone. Then the assailant leaped from the box to the stage, twelve feet below. One of his boot spurs caught on the regimental flag draped over the box. As he crashed onto the stage, he broke the shinbone of his left leg.

The assailant struggled to his feet, faced the audience, and shouted the motto of the commonwealth of Virginia: *"Sic semper tyrannis"*—(Thus always to tyrants). The stunned and disbelieving audience recognized him as John Wilkes Booth, the well-known actor. What was going on? Was this part of the play?

Booth hobbled offstage and out the stage door, where a horse was saddled and waiting. Twelve days later he would be cornered by federal troops and shot in a Virginia barn.

The theatre was in an uproar. People were shouting, standing on chairs, shoving for the exits, as Laura Keene cried out from the stage, "The president is shot! The president is shot!" ❖

✳ What did you find important in this selection? Fill in the chart.

Important details	Key sentences	Key words and phrases

✳ Think about the ideas in the chart above. What's a good main idea for this selection?

....

....

....

Thinking about the ideas, sentences, and words can help you determine the most important details in a text.

....

....

....

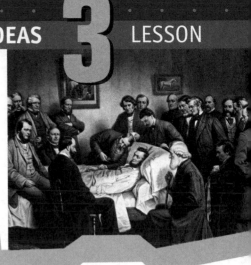

Learning more information about a topic can change the way you think about it. As you continue to read about Abraham Lincoln, you'll discover more details about his assassination.

As you read, think about how the new information changes your thoughts and ideas. Underline details that surprise you or change your thinking. Write any questions or comments in the **Response Notes**.

from Lincoln: A Photobiography
by Russell Freedman

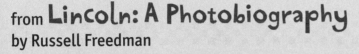

Response Notes

Two doctors rushed to the president's box. Lincoln had lost consciousness instantly. The bullet had entered his skull above his left ear, cut through his brain, and lodged behind his right eye. The doctors worked over him as Mary hovered beside them, sobbing hysterically. Finally, six soldiers carried the president out of the theatre and across the fog-shrouded street to a boardinghouse, where a man with a lighted candle stood beckoning. He was placed on a four-poster bed in a narrow room off the hallway. The bed wasn't long enough for Lincoln. He had to be laid diagonally across its cornhusk mattress.

Five doctors worked over the president that night. Now and then he groaned, but it was obvious that he would not regain consciousness. The room filled with members of the cabinet, with congressmen and high government officials. Mary waited in the front parlor. "Bring Tad—he will speak to Tad—he loves him so," she cried. Tad had been attending another play that evening. Sobbing, "They killed my pa, they killed my pa," he was taken back to the White House to wait.

Robert Lincoln was summoned to join the hushed crowd around his father's bedside. Outside, cavalry patrols clattered down the street. Another assassin had just tried to murder Secretary of State William Seward.

Everyone suspected that the attacks were part of a rebel conspiracy to murder several government officials and capture the city.

By dawn, a heavy rain was falling. Lincoln was still breathing faintly. Robert Lincoln surrendered to tears, then others in the room began to cry. At 7:22 A.M. on April 15, Lincoln died at the age of fifty-six. A doctor folded the president's hands across his chest. Gently he smoothed Lincoln's contracted face muscles, closed his eyelids, and drew a white sheet over his head. It was then that Secretary of War Edwin M. Stanton murmured, "Now he belongs to the ages." ❖

✳ **What new information did you learn about Lincoln's assassination?**

✳ **With a partner, discuss the new information you learned. What did you learn from your partner?**

※ Write a newspaper article announcing Lincoln's assassination to the country. Include the information you think is important.

Lincoln Is Assassinated
April 15, 1865

....

....

....

....

....

....

....

....

....

....

....

....

As you learn more about a topic, notice how your thoughts and ideas change.

Think about a fiction story you have read recently. What do you remember about it? Who were the characters? In fiction, what characters do and say can help you figure out an important point the author is trying to make.

This selection is from the novel *Miracle's Boys*. As you read, notice what the main character says and does. Underline sentences, words, and phrases that describe his thoughts and actions. In the **Response Notes**, write about why the underlined text is important.

Response Notes

from Miracle's Boys by Jacqueline Woodson

Ty'ree was all right after Mama died. But I was all wrong. The year before, I'd seen this show about snakes. They showed this one snake slipping out of its old skin and then leaving that old skin on the ground behind him. That's how I felt—like Mama'd been my skin. But I hadn't grown a new skin underneath, like that snake had. I was just blood and bones spreading all over the place. Every night Ty'ree stayed with me in my room till I cried myself to sleep. And the next morning he'd find me sleeping curled up on the floor beside his bed.

After a few weeks of me ending up on the floor, he called Aunt Cecile, and she came back to New York and asked around trying to find a doctor I could go to—a psychologist. Some afternoons I'd come home from school to find Aunt Cecile sitting at the dining room table writing down and crossing out numbers as she talked on the phone. And some evenings I'd catch her and Ty'ree whispering about different doctors, their fees, and social service benefits.

Then one afternoon Aunt Cecile announced that she'd found a person I could talk to named Dr. Vernon. That Wednesday and for a whole lot of Wednesdays after that, Aunt Cecile would take me to Dr. Vernon—an old man with a nice office in Harlem. His office was all wood and windows and smelled like heat and dust and warm blankets. Smells I'd always liked. So while Aunt Cecile sat in the waiting room, I went into Dr. Vernon's office. I wasn't afraid, 'cause the warm blanket smell felt like it was covering me up, protecting me.

The first time I went to Dr. Vernon, he put some paper and some markers on his desk and asked me to draw a picture for him. There was a little table in the corner, and he told me I could sit there and draw for as long as I liked. But I didn't want to draw. I sat at that table for a long time just feeling the warm blanket around me and staring at that blank white paper and those markers until Dr. Vernon told me it was okay to go.

The second time I went, Dr. Vernon gave me the paper and the markers again. I wrote my name in blue. *Lafayette Miguel Bailey.* Then I wrote Ty'ree's whole name, which is Ty'ree Alfonso Bailey. And Charlie's name, Charles Javier Bailey. I stared at the paper until Dr. Vernon came over to see. He was tall and thin the way Ty'ree said my daddy had been. But Dr. Vernon's hair was white like Aunt Cecile's. And he had a white beard—a skinny black Santa Claus. I stared at the paper, and I could feel him standing above me staring down at it, too.

"That's your family," he said.

I shrugged.

"Any other members?"

I shook my head.

"How does that make you feel?" Dr. Vernon asked.

I shrugged again. "Like nothing."

"You feel like you're nothing, Lafayette?"

"No. I know I'm something. I'm just saying that not having a mama and a daddy don't feel like nothing. It's just the way things are."

"And how does that make you feel?" he asked again.

I stared down at the paper, at me and my brothers' names. It was a lot of white space where there wasn't any writing. I had tried to write our names real big, but they still looked small, almost like nothing against all that white.

"I want my mama back," I whispered.

Dr. Vernon patted me on the shoulder and said, "I know you do, Lafayette." ❖

✳ Look back over the selection and your Response Notes. Find two actions or interactions involving the main character. For each one, what important idea did you learn?

Main character's action or interaction

Important idea you learned

● ● ● ●

● ● ● ●

✳ What connections do you make with this selection?

....

....

....

....

....

✳ How do your connections help you decide what is important to you?

....

....

....

....

....

✳ How is Lafayette working to maintain his balance?

....

....

....

....

....

Important ideas can often be found in a character's words and actions.

In fiction, **dialogue** often reveals important points the author is trying to make. In this continuation of *Miracle's Boys*, you'll read a dialogue between Lafayette and Dr. Vernon. Listen for important ideas in the lines the characters say. Underline sentences, words, or phrases that tell important points the author is trying to make. In your **Response Notes**, write why the underlined text is important.

Response Notes

from Miracle's Boys by Jacqueline Woodson

We stayed like that a long time—me staring down at the paper, Dr. Vernon softly patting my shoulder. We didn't say anything. There wasn't anything to say. After a long while had passed, Dr. Vernon said, "You can go now, Lafayette."

But I didn't want to go. I liked the way it felt to have Dr. Vernon patting my shoulder. I liked how deep and soft his voice was. So I came back. Every Wednesday for a whole year. And while Dr. Vernon stood above me or sat beside me, I drew pictures and told him what I remembered and what I wished for. I told him about the hairy hands that came at my throat in the middle of the night, the hands that wanted to choke me for not saving Mama. And how the only way I could keep them away from me was to go into Mama's room, where she was waiting for me, where she told me to lie down and go to sleep, that everything would be all right soon.

"What does 'all right' mean, Lafayette?" Dr. Vernon asked me one Wednesday. By then Aunt Cecile had long gone back down south, and I took the train by myself. I'd gotten used to the train ride, to Dr. Vernon's wood-and-window office, to his soft voice telling me all the things I'd done right in my life and how it wasn't my fault Mama had died.

I looked down at the picture I'd been drawing. It was a picture of me and Ty'ree walking together down our block. Ty'ree had his hand around my shoulder and was smiling. I had my hands in my pockets and was looking up at him.

I held the picture up so Dr. Vernon could get a closer look at it. "This," I said, feeling a smile coming on.

"If you're scared at night—" Dr. Vernon began, but I didn't let him finish.

"Then Ty'ree's there for me. Ty'ree and Mama."

"Where's your mama, Lafayette?" Dr. Vernon asked softly. His white eyebrows crinkled, and he looked at me like he was searching my face for something.

"She died," I whispered. "I know that. But I still feel her."

"Where?"

"Everywhere."

I looked at Dr. Vernon. It was almost time to go. He'd told me a while back that this would be my last visit with him, that I'd done all the work I needed to do here. He said I was gonna be okay.

Dr. Vernon smiled and patted my shoulder. "You can go now, Lafayette. Maybe I'll see you around sometime."

"Yeah," I said. When I got to the door, I turned to him and waved good-bye, then ran back over and hugged him hard. "Maybe," I said. ❖

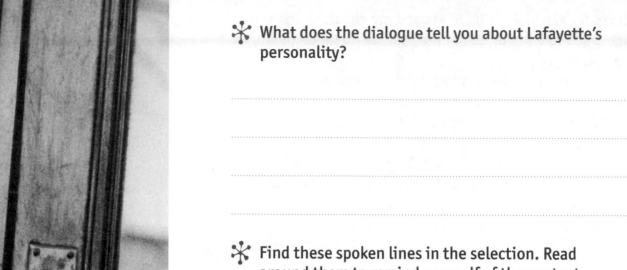

✳ What does the dialogue tell you about Lafayette's personality?

....

....

....

....

✳ Find these spoken lines in the selection. Read around them to remind yourself of the context. What important ideas do they tell you?

Excerpt from dialogue	What important idea does it tell you?
"What does 'all right' mean, Lafayette?"	
"Where's your mama, Lafayette?"	
"You can go now, Lafayette. Maybe I'll see you around sometime."	

✳ Write a short dialogue about one of these situations. Have the characters tell a story through their words. Try to reveal important ideas through the dialogue.

■ On the school bus, Nina asks Hector what is in the big box he is carrying.

■ On the playground, Justin asks Danielle how she likes her new braces.

....

....

....

....

....

....

....

....

....

....

....

....

....

....

....

Important ideas can often be found in conversations between characters.

Nonfiction texts are sometimes organized into short sections. Each section can have its own title, or **heading**. A heading gives you a clue about what the important ideas will be in that section.

This selection tells about one of the worst oil spills in history. Read each heading carefully. As you read, underline sentences, words, or phrases that answer the question in the heading. In your **Response Notes**, write any questions or comments you have.

Response Notes

from **After the Spill** by Sandra Markle

What Happened Here?

Imagine the mess if you punched a can opener into the bottom of an aluminum can full of soda. Now, imagine ripping a hole in the bottom of a ship full of oil—a ship that's longer than three football fields and extends down into the water as far as an upside-down five-story building.

That's what happened just seconds after midnight on March 24, 1989. Crossing Prince William Sound to the Pacific Ocean, the crewman on duty spotted ice ahead and turned the *Exxon Valdez* out of the ship's normal route. Too big to turn easily, the ship went far off course and struck Bligh Reef, a jumble of jagged boulders just twelve meters (forty feet) below the water's surface. The rocks ripped open the ship's metal hull.

What happened next was a disaster. Cleaning up the mess cost several billion dollars and has taken years.

Why Was This Spill Such a Big Problem?

Aleyska, the company responsible for transporting the oil, was called within minutes of the wreck, but the spill took everyone by surprise. Nobody had thought such a big oil spill would ever happen, so Aleyska was caught unprepared. Although workers at Aleyska knew how to handle an ordinary spill, there weren't enough resources to clean up after the *Exxon Valdez*.

Besides being large, the Exxon Valdez spill was difficult to clean because of its remote location. The only way to reach the spill was by helicopter or boat.

Because the weather was clear and the sea was very calm, Aleyska officials thought the oil would just stay pooled around the shipwreck. For three days, the company's spill experts tested different plans to find the best way to clean up the spill. Then something unexpected happened. A fierce storm with high winds created strong waves that pushed the oil away from the wreck and onto the beaches. Now the mess was a disaster.

What Happened to the Animals?

This bird didn't expect oil to be floating on the water when it landed on the waves in search of a fish dinner. Its feathers immediately became coated with the oil, which let cold water reach the bird's skin. When the bird tried to clean its feathers by pulling them through its mouth, it was poisoned by swallowing the toxic oil. Many seabirds, such as cormorants and scoters, died from getting too cold or swallowing the oil.

Volunteers picked up and cleaned as many of the birds as they could, but it was a difficult process. An oily bird had to be dunked in warm soapy water while the feathers were scrubbed with a toothbrush to loosen the sticky oil. Then the soap had to be rinsed away. Usually the whole process needed to be repeated a second time. Sadly, this cleaning was stressful for the birds, and many of those that were rescued died in the process.

Sea otters were victims of the *Exxon Valdez* oil spill too. When an otter swam into the oil or popped up through the slick to take a breath of air, it became coated with the sticky black stuff. Just like seabirds, sea otters depend on their fluffy coat to stay warm. Their fur traps air warmed by their body heat close to their skin. Matted with oil, the fur can no longer do its job. Naturally, the oil-coated otters tried to clean themselves the only way they knew how: by licking their fur. So they too were poisoned by swallowing the toxic oil.

Picking up oiled otters, cleaning them, and moving them to unoiled beaches took a lot of time, effort, and money. Experts at Exxon estimated that it cost about $80,000 each to rescue and clean the sea otters. Kathy Frost, of the Alaska Department of Fish and Game, reported that, sadly, many of the cleaned otters died anyway.

How Are the Animals Today?

What about the animals that live in or around Prince William Sound? Have they recovered from the oil spill? The answer depends on the kind of animal.

It's uncertain whether the sea otter population will recover from the spill, but success depends in part on the recovery of their habitat. For sea otters to do well, the populations of the fish, crabs, and snails that they eat must recover too. The key is the recovery of brown seaweed in the area just offshore. The large leaves of the adult plants are home to snails and limpets and shelter young fish. Besides being oiled, the brown seaweed was killed by the high-pressure, hot-water wash used to clean the beaches. This just goes to show that anything that disrupts an environment hurts the whole web of life living there. ❖

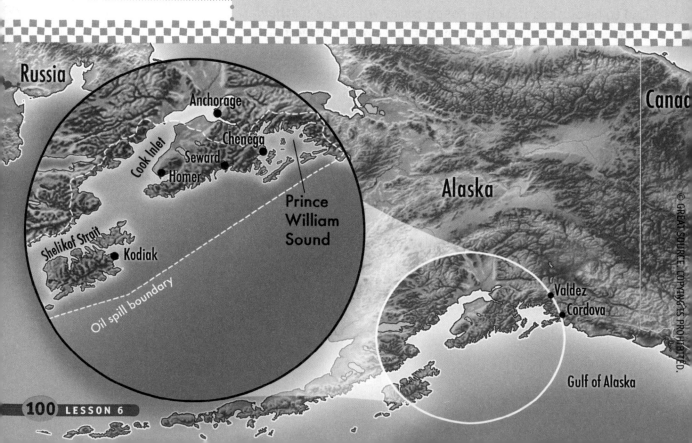

✳ Look back over the selection and your Response Notes. What are the big ideas in each section? Start by looking at the smaller details. Then figure out the big idea.

Heading	A few important details	What's the big idea?
What Happened Here?		
Why Was This Spill Such a Big Problem?		
What Happened to the Animals?		
How Are the Animals Today?		

✳ What questions do you still have about the *Exxon Valdez* oil spill?

....

....

....

....

....

....

✳ How do you think the spill affected the land animals, the people in the area, and the shoreline?

....

....

....

....

....

....

....

Headings give you clues about the important ideas in a section.

Authors sometimes use humor to express important ideas about story characters. As you read the passage from the novel *My Life as a Fifth-Grade Comedian*, look for the humor in the characters' words. What important ideas do you learn about the characters? Do you learn anything serious about either character? Serious ideas are often hidden in humor.

As you read, underline both funny and important ideas in the text. In the **Response Notes**, write why you think the ideas are important.

from My Life as a Fifth-Grade Comedian by Elizabeth Levy

Mr. Matous can be pretty funny. He *likes* to laugh. Some teachers don't, but when you get one who does, you're golden. It's Mr. Matous's first year of teaching. He's the kind of teacher who thinks all kids are worth saving. Everybody in the class knows that I am the type of kid who is too much for Mr. Matous to handle. It's made for an interesting year.

"Hand your homework assignments up to the front," said Mr. Matous. My classmates were smirking. I could tell they were just waiting for what I would do next. I wouldn't disappoint them. I always come up with something. One by one, my classmates gave their homework to Mr. Matous—everyone except me. "Bobby," said Mr. Matous. He sounded tired. "Did you do your homework?"

"No," I admitted. "I did some other kid's homework."

The class tittered. "Bobby, that joke is so old, it has mold on it," said Mr. Matous.

The class laughed hysterically. That's what I love about Mr. Matous. He's as funny as I am. "Quiet!" he shouted. "It wasn't that funny. Bobby, this is the third time in a row that you haven't done your homework. What's the problem?"

Response Notes

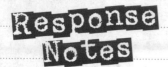
"It's not a good time in my life for homework right now." The class cracked up again.

"Now what exactly does that mean?" asked Mr. Matous.

"I mean, there's a lot going on at home right now. I don't have time for homework."

Mr. Matous looked confused. I tend to have that effect on teachers. "Class, open your history books and review the chapter on Columbus's first encounters with Native Americans," he said. He came down the aisle and stood in front of my desk with a concerned look on his face. "What's happening at home that's keeping you from doing your homework?" he asked softly. "If there's really a problem, you know that you can come to me."

I thought about it. First-year teachers are such suckers for hard-luck stories. I could tell him about Jimmy's fight with my parents after he got kicked out of school. I looked out the window. It was a cold March day. I was supposed to meet Jimmy after school. Jimmy's almost eighteen— eight years older than me. He's staying with a friend. I miss him. Home is not exactly a barrel of laughs without Jimmy. He left home, and my parents won't ask him back. They call it tough love, but it seems like tough luck to me. I can just imagine what will happen to me when I step out of line. The wind was blowing. A gust of wind hit a piece of newspaper and sent it tumbling up into the air—as if the laws of gravity had been turned upside down.

"What problems?" repeated Mr. Matous.

"Uh, seriously, Mr. Matous," I said in a loud voice so the other kids could hear, "I would have done my homework, but there was a problem in my house. They cut off the gravity. Dad forgot to pay the bill. He's very absentminded."

I could hear some of my classmates giggling. It was a sound I loved.

"Cut off the gravity," repeated Mr. Matous. Most adults would ask, "Is that supposed to be a joke?" Not Mr. Matous. He was having a hard time keeping a straight face.

"Yeah, things are pretty up in the air right now." I love it when jokes come to me. I'd have to add this one to my notebook. I write down the best jokes that I've heard or made up. I've got a whole shelf full of books on how to be a comic, and they all say the same thing—keep a notebook

with you at all times to jot down ideas. But this idea was more than just a joke. I wished something like that could really happen—gravity cutting off. All my problems would float up and away. ❖

✳ What important ideas did you learn about the two characters? Fill in the chart.

Important ideas about Mr. Matous	Important ideas about Bobby

✳ What do you think is the funniest part of this passage? What do you think is the most serious part of this passage? Explain.

....

....

....

....

....

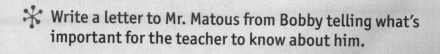

✳ Write a letter to Mr. Matous from Bobby telling what's important for the teacher to know about him.

The serious side of humor can tell you important details about a character.

An **interview** is a direct way to learn about a person. You often learn important personal details about the interviewee. Knowing personal details can help you better connect with and understand the person being interviewed.

You will read an excerpt from an interview with Mario Molina, a famous scientist. Mario Molina was born in Mexico City, one of the most polluted cities in the world. As a child, he loved science. He never stopped learning about it. In fact, he is now an expert in the science of pollution. He was even awarded a Nobel Prize in Chemistry.

As you read, think about these questions: What are the most important details that you learn about Molina's childhood? What does Molina teach you about the qualities a scientist has? Underline sentences and phrases that show important ideas. In the **Response Notes**, write about why they're important to you.

from an Interview with Mario Molina

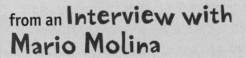

Q Were you interested in science when you were young?

A When I was in elementary school, I was very interested in science already. I must have been ten or eleven years old. I started experiments with chemistry sets at my home in Mexico. I was able to borrow a bathroom and convert it to a laboratory. My parents supported it. They were pleased. My friends just tolerated it. It was very thrilling to find out how nature works. I remember playing with toy microscopes. I discovered I could see all sorts of life, like a drop of water that had been in contact with pesticides. I could see all kinds of creatures that were moving but that seemed invisible.

Q Did you have any role models when you were growing up?

A Not at the beginning but a little later in high school, some of my teachers were role models. Also, I had an aunt

© GREAT SOURCE. COPYING IS PROHIBITED.

who was a chemist. We did scientific experiments that went beyond toy chemistry sets. She was a role model for me.

Q Do you remember the first experiment that you performed?

A For the first experiment, I did chemical analysis of stuff around the house, of whatever I could find. I did it to find out what the chemicals in it were. Sometimes it turned out to be very difficult. I took cleaning powder and sometimes food to analyze.

Q Did your friends think your interest in science was weird?

A Initially they did because they thought it was homework. It's not something that you usually do to enjoy yourself. But I explained to them that for me, it was very, very interesting, and I had a lot of fun. I think they understood then.

Q What qualities do you need to become a scientist?

A First of all, you need curiosity. You want to find out how things work. You also need creativity—to want to find out new things, the things that are not discovered yet in nature. You have to have patience and perseverance, and you need to work hard. But perhaps most importantly, you have to enjoy what you do. Then you will do it very well.

Q What do you think is the worst threat to the earth's environment?

A That's a difficult question, but I can name a few. Global warming is one. We are adding acids to the atmosphere. That will change the climate in the world. Another important problem is the burning down of forests all over the world. This problem is causing many animals and plants to disappear because we are taking away these forests. There are also worries about water that we need to grow food. It's polluted in many places.

Q Can we find solutions to such big problems?

A Yes, we can, but it is not going to be easy.

[Q] Do you think people can overcome [their] greed and solve these big environmental problems?

[A] I am an optimist. I am positive. It's possible to do the necessary changes, but it's not going to be easy. It will take a lot of hard work. I have a lot of trust in the children now, in young people. I think they are paying more and more attention to the problems of our planet. That's the big hope I have. I think the children can do better than we did. ❖

❋ What are three important details about Molina's childhood?

1. ....

2. ....

3. ....

Combine the three details above to create one big idea that tells about Molina's childhood.

....

....

❋ All the selections in this unit are about maintaining balance. How does this interview connect with that idea? Choose one more selection from this unit and answer the same question.

Name of selection	How is it connected with "maintaining balance"?
Interview with Mario Molina	

✳ As a reader, how do you make choices about what ideas are important in a text?

✳ Why does learning new information sometimes change your feelings about what is important in a text?

In an interview, look for important ideas in personal details.

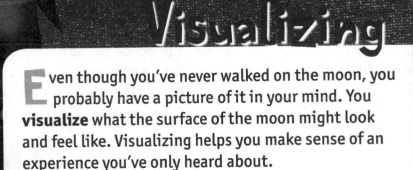

Visualizing

Even though you've never walked on the moon, you probably have a picture of it in your mind. You **visualize** what the surface of the moon might look and feel like. Visualizing helps you make sense of an experience you've only heard about.

You can visualize as you read, too. Words and descriptions that appeal to your five senses can help you visualize images and feelings. These **sensory images** can make it easier for you to remember and understand the texts you read.

The selections in this unit focus on **differences**— both in people's daily life and in the natural world. As you read about differences, you'll practice visualizing to help you understand the texts more fully.

Poets often use strong verbs, specific nouns, and comparisons to create images in readers' minds. When you **visualize**, or create a mental image, of what the poet describes, you can better understand and appreciate the poem you are reading.

   The poem you will read is called "Aquarium." As you read, notice the words that help you visualize the different sea animals. Underline comparisons that the poet makes and strong verbs that he uses. Draw images and write your thoughts in the **Response Notes**.

Response Notes

I like the sound of

those three verbs.

That comparison helps

me see sharp teeth.

Aquarium by X. J. Kennedy

1 Flashes of fishes, quick flicks of tails.
2 <u>Scoot scurry scamper</u> of scattering scales.
3 A sponge blows bubbles, sea horses race,
4 Anemones wave tentacles of slow pink lace.

5 A whale of a sailfish unfolds a fin,
6 Fans a whiskery walrus with a double chin.
7 A shovelhead shark grins, his mouth underneath
8 <u>Like a cave full of stalactites—steel-knife teeth.</u>

9 The ocean brims over with creatures, it seems,
10 That swim past my eyes like remembered dreams.
11 From behind glass, a couple of curious squid
12 Stare out at me: *What's that odd thing—a kid?* ❖

✳ Choose four short phrases from the poem that create images in your mind. Write the phrases below. Then choose your favorite and draw the image it makes you see.

1. "... sponge blows bubbles"

2.

3.

4.

Favorite phrase:

※ Look at the comparison in lines 7–8. Draw a picture that shows the sensory image this comparison creates.

SIMILE

A comparison like the one in lines 7–8 is called a **simile**. Authors use similes to show how two very different things are alike in one particular way. Similes often contain the words *like* or *as*.

Examples:

He ran as fast as a cheetah.

The sidewalk was like a skating rink.

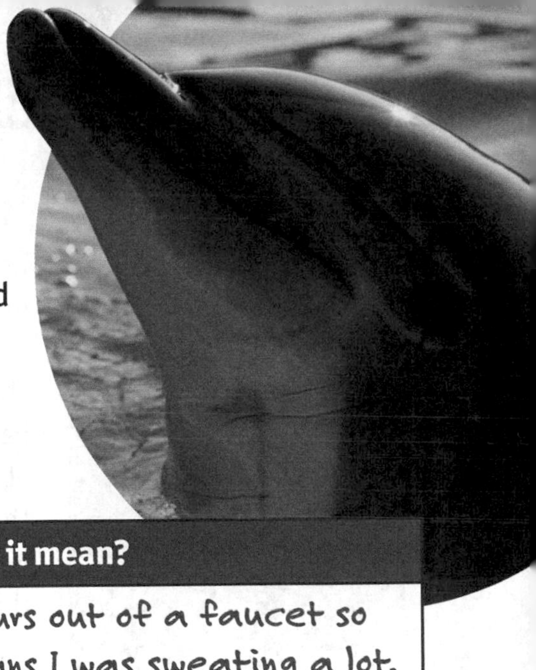

✳ Read the topic phrases. What sensory images come to mind? Use the phrases to spark ideas for three similes. Use the words *like* or *as*. Make up your own topics if you prefer.

being nervous

running fast

feeling cold

hearing a loud sound

hearing a quiet sound

eating spicy food

lying in the hot sun

Your simile	What does it mean?
Before the audition, I sweat like a faucet.	Water pours out of a faucet so that means I was sweating a lot.

Visualize sensory images to help you imagine the writer's words.

When you read about something new or confusing, it is often helpful to **visualize**. Picturing the new information in your mind may help you better understand it.

Letter from a Concentration Camp is **historical fiction**. The letter is made-up, but it's based on events that really happened. The setting is World War II, when the United States was at war with Germany, Italy, and Japan. During that time, the U.S. government feared that Japanese Americans would become spies for Japan. As a result, the U.S. government forced tens of thousands of Japanese Americans to live as prisoners in internment camps. Years later, the U.S. government admitted its mistake and apologized to the Japanese American community.

As you read, underline details or descriptions that are new or confusing. In the **Response Notes**, write questions you have and sketch the images you see.

Response Notes

Letter from a Concentration Camp
by Yoshiko Uchida

Dear Hermie:

Here I am sitting on an army cot in a smelly old horse stall, where Mama, Bud, and I have to live for who knows how long. It's pouring rain, the wind's blowing in through all the cracks, and Mama looks like she wants to cry. I guess she misses Papa. Or maybe what got her down was that long, muddy walk along the racetrack to get to the mess hall for supper.

Anyway, now I know how it feels to stand in line at a soup kitchen with hundreds of hungry people. And that cold potato and weiner they gave me sure didn't make me feel much better. I'm still hungry, and I'd give you my last nickel if you appeared this minute with a big fat hamburger and a bagful of cookies.

You know what? It's like being in jail here—not being free to live in your own house, do what you want, or eat what you want. They've got barbed wire all around this racetrack and guard towers at each corner to make sure we can't get out. Doesn't that sound like a prison? It sure feels like one!

What I want to know is, What am I doing here anyway? *Me*—a genuine born-in-California citizen of the United States of America stuck behind barbed wire, just because I *look* like the enemy in Japan. And how come you're not in here too, with that German blood in your veins and a name like Herman Schnabel. We're at war with Germany too, aren't we? And with Italy? What about the people at Napoli Grocers?

My brother, Bud, says the U.S. government made a terrible mistake that they'll regret someday. He says our leaders betrayed us and ignored the Constitution. But you know what I think? I think war makes people crazy. Why else would a smart man like President Franklin D. Roosevelt sign an executive order to force us Japanese Americans out of our homes and lock us up in concentration camps? Why else would the FBI take Papa off to a POW camp just because he worked for a Japanese company? Papa—who loves America just as much as they do.

Hey, ask Mrs. Wilford what that was all about. I mean that stuff she taught us in sixth grade about the Bill of Rights and due process of law. If that means everybody can have a hearing before being thrown in prison, how come nobody gave us a hearing? I guess President Roosevelt forgot about the Constitution when he ordered us into concentration camps. I told you war makes people crazy!

Well, Hermie, I gotta go now. Mama says we should get to the showers before the hot water runs out like it did when she went to do the laundry. Tomorrow she's getting up at 4:00 A.M. to beat the crowd. Can you imagine having to get up in the middle of the night and stand in line to wash your sheets and towels? By hand too! No luxuries like washing machines in this dump!

Hey, do me a favor? Go pet my dog, Rascal, for me. He's probably wondering why I had to leave him with Mrs. Harper next door. Tell him I'll be back to get him for sure. It's just that I don't know when. There's a rumor we're

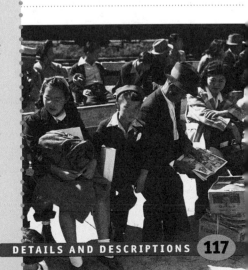

getting shipped to some desert—probably in Utah. But don't worry, when this stupid war is over, I'm coming home to California and nobody's ever going to kick me out again! You just wait and see! So long, Hermie.

Your pal,
Jimbo Kurasaki ❖

✳ Jimbo says, "I told you war makes people crazy!" List some of Jimbo's reasons for drawing this conclusion.

....

....

....

....

✳ Illustrate a part of the letter that you connected with. Then write a detailed caption for it.

....

....

....

✳ Plan and write a letter to Jimbo expressing how his letter makes you feel.

Date: ....

Dear Jimbo,

Your friend, ...

Visualizing new or confusing information will help you better understand it.

Authors often include the five senses in their writing—sight, sound, taste, smell, and touch (or how something feels)—to help you create sensory images. The more you can "see," the more you will understand and enjoy an author's work.

In this excerpt from the novel *A Small White Scar,* Will is running away from home on horseback. Notice how the author uses a lot of sensory descriptions but focuses more on one sense than the others. Can you figure out which one?

As you read, underline the descriptions that appeal to your senses. In the **Response Notes**, write about the senses you notice.

Response Notes

from A Small White Scar by K. A. Nuzum

Moonlight still dusted the top of the mesa as Deep and I climbed onto the flat. As his weight came over each back leg, I felt the saddlebags and my bedroll shift slightly on his rump. I took a long, slow breath of the last of the night air and reined in, turning Deep so we faced the ranch one last time. It was pitch-black. My father had left only the day before with three hands and two hundred fifty head of cattle, and already Milton the cook was taking advantage and sleeping late. Hank would have him up shortly, though. And that meant Denny would get up too. He'd wonder where I was, but he wouldn't think of the words to say right off. After a while, maybe after breakfast, he'd all of a sudden go up to Hank and ask, "Where is Will? Where is brother Will?"

I gripped the reins tighter and swung Deep away from home. My knees were weak as I pressed them against his sides. He burst into a fast lope across the top of the mesa, but Denny's words and then my father's chased us.

"Son, look after your brother."

That was always the last thing my father said to me, as it had been at dawn the day before when he shook my hand and set out on the cattle drive. I had been dragging those words around like a leg trap ever since my mother's death seven long years ago. "Look after your brother" started out meaning different things to me and my father. When he said it, he meant keep Denny out of his hair so he didn't have to worry with him.

I thought "look after your brother" meant help him grow up, help him be a person. I thought that till I was nine. ✣

✳ All the passages in the chart refer to one sense. Which sense is it? Add another sensory passage to the chart. Then write the sense it appeals to.

Passage	Sense
"As his weight came over each back leg, I felt the saddlebags and my bedroll shift slightly on his rump."	
"I gripped the reins tighter and swung Deep away from home."	
"My knees were weak as I pressed them against his sides."	

✳ Choose a sentence or phrase from the selection that you visualize well. Write it on the lines. Then draw the image you see.

....

....

✳ What connections do you make with the main character, Will? Explain.

....

....

....

....

....

Use all five senses to create images when you read.

What is one of the most memorable moments of your life? Chances are, there's a strong feeling attached to it—perhaps happiness, fear, excitement, sadness, confusion, or pride.

When an author describes strong feelings in a part of a story, that part is often easy to remember. Strong feelings make strong mental images.

The excerpt from the novel *A Small White Scar* continues below. Will is remembering when he tried to teach his twin brother, Denny, to read. Denny has Down syndrome and had a hard time learning.

As you read, underline sentences and phrases that show strong feelings. In the **Response Notes**, write about the feelings the characters are experiencing and the sensory images you create.

from **A Small White Scar** by K. A. Nuzum

I thought "look after your brother" meant help him grow up, help him be a person. I thought that till I was nine. Until Denny and I were nine, and we decided it was time for him to learn to read. I spent days and days going over my old primer with him, getting him to where he could point to every word under every picture as he said it.

"'The tree is green.' 'The wagon is red.' 'The flower is lellow.'"

When he'd done it perfectly six times in a row, we decided to show off to our father.

Denny raced through every page, all the way through the picture of the blue house.

Then he paused. His mouth dropped open, his eyebrows jumped high on his forehead. His eyes, full up with just one question, lifted to our father.

Our father nodded.

"That's real fine, Denny."

Denny's face lit up like a brush fire.

My father reached out and flipped back several pages

Response Notes

in the book. "Read me this page again, why don't you." Denny beamed at my father's interest. He stared at the picture of a small, black dog sitting up and begging.

He looked down at the words.

His lips pursed.

My heart pounded.

Denny pointed to the first word. "This."

Pointed to the second. "Is."

I dropped my head.

"A black puppy dog." His index finger jabbed at the words.

Our father stepped closer to Denny and skimmed his fingers beneath each word. "'The dog is black.' That's what it says, son. What you did was memorize the book, the order of the pages."

All the light had gone out of Denny's face and he shuffled off, and our father lit into me about how I was damaging Denny by setting his hopes too high.

"Feebleminded," he said. "He'll never read. Don't try to make him something he can't be. Take care of your brother. Look after him."

It took me a while to figure it out, but by the time I was twelve or so, I knew the only way I could ever escape the trap of those words was to chew my leg off just like a coyote would in order to free himself. That is what I had done.

Soon we were five miles distant from the ranch, and Deep's hooves ate up another two mighty quick. In four more the edge of the mesa was coming up fast, and while I knew every inch of the mesa's top, and felt fine riding Deep at a dead run over it on the darkest night, its slopes were treacherous and ever-changing. I slowed Deep to a walk, and we started down the far side of the Mesa de Maya.

The last star had quietly left the sky; a new day was showing up all pink and gold in the east. Maybe, just maybe, everything would turn out. My belly was grinding; I was starving. I reached back to one of the saddlebags and pulled out a fistful of jerky.

Getting food in my belly made me feel steadier, and I let more thoughts slide into my head a little bit at a time.

I was headed into the future.

I had decided I would have a future. ❖

✳ How do you think each character feels when Denny reads for Will and their father? How do you feel? In the chart, write about your feelings and images.

Character	How each person feels	The sensory images you create
Denny		
Father		
Will		
You		

✳ Why is Will leaving? Why does he think he can't have a future at home?

....

....

....

....

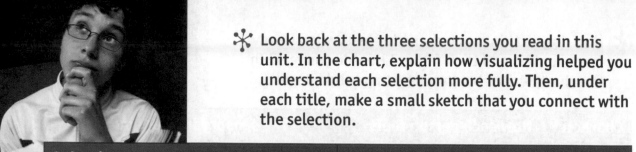

Look back at the three selections you read in this unit. In the chart, explain how visualizing helped you understand each selection more fully. Then, under each title, make a small sketch that you connect with the selection.

Selection	How did you use visualizing to help you understand the selection?
"Aquarium"	
Letter from a Concentration Camp	
A Small White Scar	

Remembering strong feelings will help you create strong sensory images.

IMAGES FROM DIALOGUE

A conversation between two people is called a **dialogue.** Dialogues often spark strong sensory images.

In this dialogue from the novel *Free Baseball,* Felix and his mother are talking about the night they fled from Cuba. Cuba is an island country ninety miles from Florida. Its government does not allow people to come and go as they please. Occasionally, Cubans try to escape to the United States by boat. It can be a dangerous journey.

As you read the dialogue, underline sentences and phrases that help you create sensory images. What senses does the author include? In the **Response Notes,** write about the images you see and the senses you notice.

from Free Baseball by Sue Corbett

Response Notes

She smiled at him, then took in a big breath. "The night we left from Cojimar, it was like this night—dark and warm. Beautiful. We had to sneak down to the beach, be absolutely quiet, and wear dark clothing so the moon wouldn't show us. When we got there, there were maybe twenty-five, thirty others, waiting to get on the boat."

"But you told me before there were thirteen people."

"*Si.* That was the problem. There was actually room on this boat for maybe six people. And all of the people on the beach had already given their money."

"So how did they decide who got to go?"

"Okay, here begins the part I have left out before, but which I think you are ready to hear, no?"

"Keep going," Felix said.

"All along, your father intended to come with us that night. He had had other chances to defect, traveling with the team. But he didn't want to be in America and have us in Cuba with no way then to get us out. And once he had defected, it would have been almost impossible for us. We would be watched, as well as punished."

"We would still be there."

"Correct. Now, the captain of this boat was only too happy to take Claudio de la Portilla—and his money—but

the person he absolutely positively didn't want to take was *you*."

"Why? What'd I do?"

"He didn't want any babies. He was insistent."

"What's wrong with babies? A baby hardly takes any space at all."

"That's true, but babies are trouble, Felix. They cry and…this is the hard part of the story for me, Felix. They can't swim. Which turned out to be important."

An image came into Felix's head. It was the dream he'd had the first night away, when he was sleeping on the clubhouse floor. The blackness, the coldness of water against his skin. "So what happened?" he asked, but he had an idea that he already knew.

"Claudio said, 'He gets MY place. And you will take them'—meaning you and me—'or you will take no one.'"

Felix leaned his head back and closed his eyes, trying to picture the scene on the beach. His strong father. His pretty mother, carrying a baby. A baby who was him.

His mother continued. "The captain finally agreed. Your father is a big star in Cuba. This puny captain couldn't refuse Claudio de la Portilla."

"So we left him there?"

"Him and a dozen others. He promised he would follow."

"But he never did." Felix put his feet up on the seat in front of him and wrapped his arms around his legs. He stared out at the field.

"He never got another chance, Felix, because…because of what happened. Because of the fuss."

"What fuss?"

"So we traveled for several hours—you were *perfecto*, Felix, not a peep out of you—but then we hit something, something in the water, rocks maybe, or debris of some kind. I never learned what it was. Water started coming in where all of us were hiding, so we went up the steps. The captain started screaming at us to go back down. He was afraid we would be detected."

"Detected?"

"By the Americans—by the Coast Guard. It was illegal, what we were doing. If you make it to Miami, they will take you as a refugee. You know that word?"

Felix nodded.

"But if they catch you in the water, they send you back to Cuba." Mami went on. "Anyway, there were life preservers on the boat, but not enough." She stopped and squeezed Felix's hand. "Is this too much for you?"

"No, don't stop."

"We got one life preserver. One for you and me—because the others knew there was no way I could try to float and hold you."

"And because of who my father was."

"*Por supuesto*, Felix. Even facing death, Cubans think about their baseball stars." ❖

✖ **Write a diary entry that shows Felix's feelings about what his mother told him.**

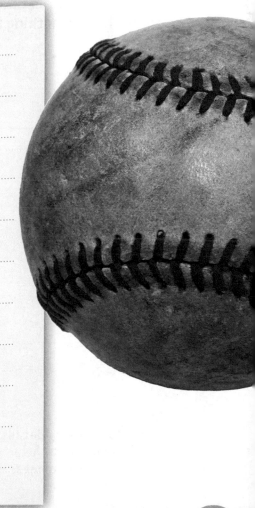

✳ The author includes sensory details for sight, sound, and touch (or how something feels). List three details from the passage that appeal to these senses.

Sense	Detail from passage
Sight	
Sound	
Touch (or how something feels)	

✳ Which is the most important detail Felix learns from his mother about the night of their escape? Why is this detail so important?

....

....

....

....

....

....

Look for sensory details in a dialogue to help you visualize images.

6 LESSON

As a plot develops, an author tells you certain details but not others. When you read, you can use what you already to know to help you create images of details and events _not_ stated by the author.

In this selection from the novel _Beetles, Lightly Toasted_, Andy is trying to learn about how to eat bugs. As you read, underline text that gives information about new events in the plot. In the **Response Notes**, write details you visualize that are not told to you by the author.

from **Beetles, Lightly Toasted**
by Phyllis Reynolds Naylor

The way Andy figured it was this: if the population ever grew so big that there wasn't enough food to feed everybody, then people could save their lives by eating things they hadn't thought of eating before. Things like lizards and snakes and grasshoppers. Not that _Andy_ would eat them, of course, but some day, if people were starving, _somebody_ might.

Start with what you have and see how far you can stretch it, Mr. Sudermann had said. _Put your imaginations to work_. Maybe you didn't have to be starving. Maybe, if you were just poor or you wanted to save money on your grocery bill, you could find stuff to eat in your own backyard.

Andy knew that primitive tribes ate things like grubs, which was just like eating worms. He had heard about fancy stores selling chocolate-covered ants as a novelty item. But no one he knew, except the yellow cat, had ever made a meal out of beetles. The first thing he had to do was find out exactly what could be eaten safely. Wendell had told him once that a university was a place where you could find out anything you wanted to know, so Andy wrote a letter to Iowa State University:

Response Notes

Dear Sir:

I am writing an essay for a contest and I need to know what bugs and things you can eat. And worms too. How do you know if they are poison or not? How do you fix them? Please answer soon.

Yours truly,
Andy Moller

On the envelope he wrote, "Department of Bugs," and then he added the address he had copied from the catalog in Wendell's room, with his own address in the corner.

Aunt Wanda saw him putting on the stamp. "Who's the letter to?" she asked, as she carried her jade plant to a sunny place on the window ledge.

"Oh, somebody," Andy told her.

"Well, most letters *are* to somebody," she said, and cast him a strange look.

Andy walked down to the end of the lane toward the mailbox. ❖

✳ Choose one event from the selection. Describe in detail the image you see in your mind. Include details that the author does not tell you.

....

....

....

....

....

....

....

✳ If someone from the Department of Bugs writes back, what will he or she say? Draft a short note here.

Date:

Dear Andy,

Your friend,

Use what you already know to help you visualize details that the author doesn't tell you.

Authors often use specific nouns to help readers create images. A specific noun names an object in a very clear way. A general noun names an object in a broad way. Look at the examples below.

- Specific nouns: salt, pepper, cinnamon

- General nouns: spices, food

The passage from *Beetles, Lightly Toasted* continues below. Andy finally gets a reply to his letter about how to eat bugs. As you read, underline specific nouns you find. Think about the mental images they help you see. In the **Response Notes**, write about or sketch the images you see.

Response Notes

from **Beetles, Lightly Toasted**

by Phyllis Reynolds Naylor

On May 1, when Andy had about given up ever hearing from the University, there was a letter for him in the box, and he was glad he had found it before anyone else did:

Dear Andy:

Your letter asking about bugs and things has been given to me for reply, and I hope I will be able to help. Probably most insects are edible, especially their larvae or pupae. But because some of them—especially brightly-colored insects—might have poisons in their bodies, it would be best to stick with crickets, grasshoppers, and ordinary brown beetles.

Ant and bee larvae are also a good source of fat and protein; meal worms, often found where grain is stored, are delicious, I understand, fried in garlic butter. To prepare insects for eating, put them on a diet of cornmeal for a few days to rid their digestive tracts of grit, then cook.

Earthworms can also be put on a diet of applesauce, then simmered until tender. Grasshoppers, crickets, and beetles, lightly toasted, with the legs and wings removed, add crunch to a recipe, and can be used in place of nuts for brownies.

If you don't like the idea of dropping live worms and insects in boiling water, you might put them in a covered box in the freezer first, then cook them later. Good luck on your essay, and *bon appetit*!

Cordially,
John Burrows, Entomologist

Andy understood the whole letter except the last two words before "cordially."

"Mom," he said that evening as he worked his arithmetic problems on the kitchen table, and she sat across from him going over her poultry and egg records, "What does *bon appetit* mean?"

"*Bon appetit*?" Mother looked up. "It's French, Andy. It means 'good appetite' or 'good eating.' 'Enjoy your meal'—something like that."

Andy kept one hand tightly over his mouth and said nothing. ✥

✳ **List five specific nouns you found.**

1. ....

2. ....

3. ....

4. ....

5. ....

✳ Write a recipe for one of the insect dishes in the letter.
Then draw a picture of it.

Recipe for

Bon appetit!

✳ If you were visiting a friend and he or she prepared a feast of toasted beetles for you, what would you do?

....

....

....

....

....

....

....

....

✳ Write a paragraph about an unusual food experience you've had.

....

....

....

....

....

....

....

....

As you read, look for specific nouns to help you visualize.

Authors often include **specific details** to help you visualize. Sometimes the details describe a time or a situation when things were very different from how they are now.

This nonfiction passage describes a time, less than forty years ago, when girls were not encouraged—or even allowed—to do many things. As you read, underline specific details that help you visualize the situations that the author describes. In the **Response Notes**, write connections you make with your own experiences.

Response Notes

from **Let Me Play** by Karen Blumenthal

Imagine a time when there were no soccer superstars like Mia Hamm or basketball heroes like Lisa Leslie. Imagine a time when people believed girls shouldn't play team sports at all, but instead should wear only dresses and act like "ladies." Imagine a time when girls were warned that hard math classes were too difficult for them and were told that a college or graduate degree was a waste of time.

Just a generation ago that was the popular thinking. Up until the 1970s there were few school teams or recreation leagues for girls outside of tennis, swimming, and track. At school, boys were encouraged to study math and science to ready them for careers. Girls were supposed to be good in English and prepare to become wives and mothers. The girls who enjoyed math, who might have become engineers or mathematicians, were urged to become teachers. Those who loved science, who dreamed of being veterinarians or doctors, were told that girls should be nurses instead.

Many of the nation's best universities didn't even accept women. Law schools and medical schools had quotas, or limits, on how many women they would take.

Then in the 1960s the civil rights movement inspired a new women's movement, and women began to speak out for fair treatment at school and in the workplace.

For me, one year stood out. As a kid in the 1960s, I had desperately wanted to play basketball. Hour after hour, I shot baskets alone in our driveway—because there was nowhere else to play. In 1972, when I was in seventh grade, a new male teacher arrived who thought girls should have a basketball team. Since hardly any of us had ever played, only seven or eight players signed up. We were short on skills but full of enthusiasm. He had to teach us everything—dribbling, defense, basic rules. In our few games we got stomped. But I loved every minute of it.

The year 1972 turned out to be pivotal for many other girls and women. The United States Congress passed several important laws to give girls and women more opportunities. The broadest was the Equal Rights Amendment (ERA), a change to the United States Constitution that would guarantee women the same rights as men. Like my basketball team, the ERA seemed full of promise. But it would face an extremely tough and ultimately unsuccessful fight to win the needed approval of three-fourths of state legislatures.

That same year Congress passed a narrow and modest little law with a bureaucratic name, Title IX. Hardly anyone knew about it, and there wasn't much to it. In a thirty-seven-word introduction, Title IX said that any school receiving money from the government couldn't treat boys and girls differently because of their sex.

Congress wanted girls to be able to take the same math classes as boys, to have a chance to become lawyers and doctors and Ph.D.'s. Before long, Title IX also came to mean that if schools sponsored sports for boys, they should sponsor them for girls, too. For the first time, girls across the United States got a real chance to play on the athletic field—and that little law took on a role far greater than anyone ever imagined it could.

No shots were fired, but a revolution followed, fought by an invisible army of committed activists, parents, coaches, and kids. Within a few short years, tens of thousands of girls were suiting up for basketball, volleyball, and soccer and pouring into colleges and graduate schools. Today, female lawyers, doctors,

and Ph.D.'s are common. Today, nearly 3 million girls play high school sports, up from only 294,000 in 1971–72. Today, we don't think twice about women playing softball in the Olympics, discovering cancer-causing genes, or serving as federal judges. In three decades Title IX truly changed the lives of girls in America. ❖

✳ **Which details from this selection create strong feelings or images for you?**

✳ Title IX was a civil rights law—a law that helped give equality to a group of citizens. Think about the selections listed below. How does the passage from *Let Me Play* connect with the two selections you read earlier in this unit?

Selection title	How does *Let Me Play* connect?
Letter from a Concentration Camp	
Free Baseball	

✳ What personal connections do you make with this passage?

....

....

....

....

❋ How does visualizing help you understand what you read?

....

....

....

....

❋ Which selection from this unit creates the most memorable sensory images for you? Explain.

....

....

....

....

❋ Look over the selections in this unit. Choose two characters and compare them. How are they alike and different?

When you read, look for specific details that help create strong sensory images.

....

....

....

Making Inferences

Suppose you're in the checkout line at a supermarket. The boy in front of you is buying dog food, dog biscuits, and a rubber bone. You imagine that the boy has a dog, even though you and the boy have never spoken. You have made an **inference.** You combined the clues you noticed with what you already know.

You can make inferences when you read, too, by combining clues in the text with what you already know. An inference can be a prediction, a conclusion, or an interpretation. Making inferences can help you discover the author's unstated meanings.

In this unit, you will read about different kinds of **relationships.** You will practice making inferences to better understand your reading.

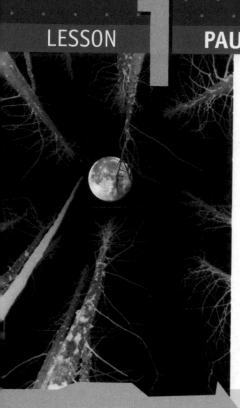

Reading is an active process. It involves pausing to think, wonder, imagine, ask questions, and reread. When you read, you bring personal meaning to the text. When you combine an unstated idea from the text with thoughts of your own experiences, you are making an **inference**. An inference can be a prediction, a conclusion, or an interpretation.

This excerpt is from a true story. In "The Night Visitors," Bryan Palmer gets lost on a hunting trip. He is alone, night has fallen, and the weather has turned cold. As you read, notice when you pause to think. In the **Response Notes**, write the predictions, conclusions, or interpretations you make. Underline details in the text that helped you make inferences.

Response Notes

Bryan must have a lot of outdoor experience because he knows how to make a fire.

from The Night Visitors by Allan Zullo

Bryan couldn't stop shivering—both from fear and from cold. *Keep walking. Don't stop. Got to keep a clear head. Man, this shotgun feels like it weighs a hundred pounds.*

Bryan's top priority had changed from finding his way back to simply surviving through the night. *I sure wish I had brought my warmer jacket. How could I have been so stupid? I've got to start a fire.*

Crouching under a thick evergreen, Bryan collected a few downed branches. He pulled out his pocket knife and whittled away the wet bark. Next he carved the dry wood underneath into paper-thin shavings. He opened a few shells and poured out the gunpowder, then tried to light the kindling with matches he was carrying in his pocket. But the mixture of wet snow and wind made it impossible.

In anger and frustration, Bryan kicked the kindling into the snow. *There's nothing else I can do. Dad's probably called for a rescue team. I better stay in one place.*

Rescue team leader Buck Mathews stood next to his search dog, a golden retriever named Goldie. She was sniffing a piece of Bryan's clothing that Carl had given them.

"We'll see if Goldie can pick up the scent and track him," said Mathews. "Carl, does your son have protective gear?"

"No."

"Then we'll head out right now. If hypothermia sets in, he could be in real danger."

In cold weather, survival depends on conserving one's body heat. Hypothermia begins when the body's temperature falls below normal, triggering uncontrollable shivering. As the body continues to chill, the shivering grows more violent. The muscles stiffen and the mind begins to break down, causing victims to say and do crazy things.

"You've got to find him soon," Carl pleaded. "There's no way Bryan can survive the night on his own."

If that happens, he might not make good choices.

✳ **Think about the story title and what you've read so far. What prediction can you make about what might happen to Bryan? Explain.**

....

....

....

It was nine o'clock and very dark. The snow continued to pile up.

They're not coming for me tonight, Bryan thought. *Maybe they'll find me in the morning. I just hope I'm still alive when they do . . . if they do.*

Sitting under the branches of the evergreen, Bryan tucked his knees to his chin and rocked back and forth in a futile effort to stay warm. *Don't fall asleep. Fight it. Fight it.*

Bryan's conversation with himself came to an abrupt end when he heard an animal snorting close by. He picked up his shotgun and loaded it. Unable to see in the dark and snow, he slid behind the tree trunk and listened.

He must be freezing!

It sounds like more than one animal. What are they? Coyotes? Wolves? Grizzlies? Well, whatever they are, they know I'm here. Maybe I can scare them.

Bryan jumped to his feet and roared, "Go away! Get outta here! Scram!" He found a few large stones and hurled them in the direction of the animals. They trotted off but returned a few minutes later. Bryan was poised to shoot, but his finger was too numb from the cold to feel the trigger. He was shaking so badly he wasn't sure he could hit anything anyway.

Bryan crept out from under the branches and peered into the snowy darkness, trying to get a better look at the animals. He lifted his shotgun, then he put it back down. A smile of relief spread across his face.

He could make out two big, gray, four-legged animals about five feet (1.5 m) tall at the shoulder. The shoulders were higher than the hindquarters, giving them a humpbacked appearance. They had short necks and long muzzles. They were female elk.

As the elk fearlessly approached the shivering teen, they lowered their heads, sniffing and studying him. For a brief moment, Bryan forgot he was lost and in danger of freezing to death. He had never seen elk that close before and stared at them in fascination. *They're not afraid of me,* he marveled.

A gust knocked snow off a branch, splattering Bryan's head. By the time he had wiped his face, the elk had gone. He huddled under the tree again, wishing he could stop shaking. He knew shivering was the first sign of hypothermia.

I should have ridden one of those elk out of here. They probably knew the way to Dad. I'm so cold . . . and so tired. Don't fall asleep . . . don't fall . . . ❖

✳ What inference can you make about what's happening to Bryan? List details to support it.

....

....

....

....

✳ What inferences can you make about how the story might end? Explain.

....

....

....

....

✳ Think about the inferences you made. How do they help you connect with the story and keep you interested?

....

....

....

....

Pause while reading to
make inferences and create
personal meaning.

You see your sister leaving for school with an umbrella. A logical inference would be that it's going to rain. So you put on your raincoat. But your sister says, "Why are you wearing a raincoat? It's not going to rain today. I have this umbrella because it's part of my costume for the school play." Your inference made sense, but it didn't fit the situation. Inferences are valuable tools for making sense of stories, articles, and real life. But sometimes the outcomes are different than you expect.

As you read the end of "The Night Visitors," notice the predictions, conclusions, and interpretations you make. Write them in the **Response Notes**. Underline the text that sparks your inferences. When you finish, revisit your inferences to see if they match the outcome.

Response Notes

from The Night Visitors by Allan Zullo

Bryan drifted off to sleep—a sleep which had the potential to kill him. But about five in the morning, he woke up on the hard ground, his muscles stiff. *I dozed off! I can't do that. I could die that way. What if the rescuers walked by when I was asleep? How stupid! Hey, I'm not shivering anymore. I feel warmer. What's that smell? It's like wet fur.*

Bryan sat up and rubbed his eyes. *I'm not dreaming this, am I? No, what I'm seeing is real—real incredible!*

To his utter amazement, both elk lay beside him, one on each side, their backs nearly touching him. *Now I see why I didn't freeze to death during the night. You two kept me warm!*

The breaking dawn revealed at least four inches of snow on the ground, but the storm was over. Seeing the elk and an end to the storm lifted Bryan's spirits. He was so grateful that he wanted to pat the sleeping animals, but he was afraid he'd startle them.

The elk began to stir, making soft, high-pitched grunts. Then they snorted and stood up. Sniffing the air, they quickly trotted off toward the north slope.

"Hey, where are you going?" shouted Bryan. "Come back. Well, thanks for keeping me warm. I couldn't have made it through the night without you."

Suddenly Bryan heard a dog barking. The barking grew louder, accompanied by a human voice coming from the woods on the other side of the meadow.

Bryan's heart leaped for joy. He scrambled to his feet and slogged through the wet snow as fast as he could. Seconds later, he spotted a golden retriever wearing a red SEARCH vest, followed by Buck Mathews.

"Over here! Over here!" Bryan shouted, wildly waving his arms and jumping up and down.

"Are you Bryan Palmer?" yelled the rescuer.

"Yes!"

"Are you all right?"

"I am now!"

Mathews checked the boy for frostbite, but there wasn't any. "Did you find shelter?"

"Not really."

"Exposure in the weather we had last night would kill anyone without shelter within a matter of hours, especially with the light clothes you have on. How did you survive?"

"Two elk saved my life."

As they returned to the command post, Bryan told Mathews the story of his late-night companions.

"Elk are very shy creatures," said Mathews. "They aren't known to approach humans. Bryan, you did suffer from hypothermia, and one of its effects is that you imagine all sorts of things. Those elk really weren't there."

"But it's true, I swear." Yet Bryan was too wet, cold, and tired to turn around and show him the proof.

After Bryan was taken to the hospital for observation, another member of the rescue team, Deputy Stan Sandberg, decided to check out the boy's story. He hiked back to the spot where Bryan had been found and followed the teen's tracks to an evergreen tree.

When Sandberg returned to the sheriff's office, he told Buck Mathews, "I found two sets of fresh elk prints leading away from the evergreen tree where Bryan stayed last night. But I didn't see any hoofprints going to the tree. That means the elk were under the tree during the snowfall.

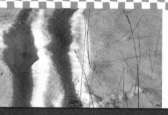

That's not all. I also found depressions in the wet ground fitting the size and shape of two elk. Buck, the kid was telling the truth!"

Meanwhile, at the hospital, Bryan told his father, "I've made an important decision. I don't ever want to go hunting again."

"Because you got lost?"

"No, that's not it. How can I possibly take the life of another wild animal after two wild animals saved my life?" ❖

✳ What are three inferences you made as you read the passage? Does each one match the outcome? Fill in the chart with your thoughts.

Inference	Does it match the outcome? Explain.

✳ Buck Mathews makes an incorrect inference about Bryan. What is the inference Buck makes, and how does he figure out it is wrong?

....

....

....

....

✳ At what point are you able to predict the final outcome of the story?

....

....

....

....

....

....

✳ Why does Bryan say he will never hunt again? Would you make the same decision? Explain the decision you would make.

....

....

....

....

Revisit your inferences to make sure they match the outcome.

When you go to a movie, you can sometimes figure out what it will be about. You do this by thinking about the title, remembering bits of information you've heard about it, and recalling similar movies you have seen. With this information, you make a **prediction** about what will happen in the movie.

You can use this skill while reading, too. Authors often "set the stage" with clues or details about what will happen next. Combine the clues with your own knowledge to make predictions about what will happen in the text.

This passage is from the nonfiction book *The Great Fire.* Underline clues and details that hint at what might happen next. Write your predictions in the **Response Notes**.

Response Notes

from The Great Fire by Jim Murphy

It was Sunday and an unusually warm evening for October eighth, so Daniel "Peg Leg" Sullivan left his stifling little house in the West Side of Chicago and went to visit neighbors. One of his stops was at the shingled cottage of Patrick and Catherine O'Leary. The one-legged Sullivan remembered getting to the O'Learys' house at around eight o'clock, but left after only a few minutes because the O'Leary family was already in bed. Both Patrick and Catherine had to be up very early in the morning: he to set off for his job as a laborer; she to milk their five cows and then deliver the milk to neighbors.

Sullivan ambled down the stretch of land between the O'Learys' and their neighbor, crossed the street, and sat down on the wooden sidewalk in front of Thomas White's house. After adjusting his wooden leg to make himself comfortable, he leaned back against White's fence to enjoy the night.

The wind coming off the prairie had been strong all day, sometimes gusting wildly, and leaves scuttled along the street; the sound of laughter and fiddle music drifted through the night. A party was going on at the McLaughlins' to celebrate the arrival of a relative from Ireland. Another neighbor, Dennis Rogan, dropped by the O'Learys' at eight-thirty, but he, too, left when he learned the family was in bed.

Fifteen minutes later, Sullivan decided to go home. As the driver of a wagon, he would need every ounce of strength come morning. It was while pushing himself up that Sullivan first saw the fire—a single tongue of flame shooting out the side of the O'Learys' barn.

Sullivan didn't hesitate a second. "FIRE! FIRE! FIRE!" he shouted as loudly as he could. Running clumsily across the dirt street, Sullivan made his way directly to the barn. There was no time to stop for help. The building was already burning fiercely and he knew that in addition to five cows, the O'Learys had a calf and a horse in there.

The barn's loft held over three tons of timothy hay, delivered earlier that day. Flames from the burning hay pushed against the roof and beams, almost as if they were struggling to break free. A shower of burning embers greeted Sullivan as he entered the building.

He untied the ropes of two cows, but the frightened animals did not move. On the other side of the barn, another cow and the horse were tied to the wall, straining to get loose. Sullivan took a step toward them, then realized that the fire had gotten around behind him and might cut off any chance of escape in a matter of seconds. The heat was fiercely intense and blinding, and in his rush to flee, Sullivan slipped on the uneven floorboards and fell with a thud.

He struggled to get up and, as he did, Sullivan discovered that his wooden leg had gotten stuck between two boards and come off. Instead of panicking, he began hopping toward where he thought the door was. Luck was with him. He had gone a few feet when the O'Learys' calf bumped into him, and Sullivan was able to throw his arms around its neck. Together, man and calf managed to find the door and safety, both frightened, both badly singed.

A shed attached to the barn was already engulfed by flames. It contained two tons of coal for the winter and

Response Notes

a large supply of kindling wood. Fire ran along the dry grass and leaves, and took hold of a neighbor's fence. The heat from the burning barn, shed, and fence was so hot that the O'Learys' house, forty feet away, began to smolder. Neighbors rushed from their homes, many carrying buckets or pots of water. The sound of music and merrymaking stopped abruptly, replaced by the shout of "FIRE!" It would be a warning cry heard thousands of times during the next thirty-one hours. ❖

✳ Look back at the selection. What do Sullivan's actions tell you? What can you infer from his actions?

Sullivan's actions	What can you infer?

✳ Look back at the predictions you made. Write two below.

✳ Which clues helped you make each prediction?

Look for clues and details in a text to help you make predictions.

LEARNING FROM A CHARACTER'S REACTION

Imagine that there is a new student in your class. How can you find out what kind of person he is? One way is to notice how he reacts to other people in the class. If he responds to questions with few words or avoids looking at others, you might conclude that he is shy. If he smiles a lot at people and starts conversations, you might conclude that he is outgoing.

You can use characters' reactions in a text to **draw conclusions** about them. *Heartbeat* is a story written in free verse. Free verse is a form of poetry without rhyming or rhythmic patterns. As you read, notice how the main character and Grandpa react to each other. Underline the text that shows you their reactions. In the **Response Notes**, write any inferences you make about their relationship. (Remember, an inference is a prediction, a conclusion, or interpretation.)

from **Heartbeat** by Sharon Creech

I am in Grandpa's room
preparing to draw my forty-fifth apple.

It perches on the glass shelf on his wall
and I am sitting on the floor
beneath it
studying it from the bottom.

Grandpa is sifting through
my fat folder of apples.

What an awful lot of apples!
he says.
They're making me hungry.

The apple on the glass shelf
does not look like an apple
from the bottom
and I don't know how I will draw it
and will it still be an apple
if it doesn't *look* like an apple? ▶

Response Notes

While I am sitting there gazing at the apple
I tell Grandpa about the coach
asking me to try out for the track team
and about Max telling me the same
and about how the coach kept bugging me
and now the tryouts are over
and the coach does not even
look me in the eye

and then I tell him about Max saying
I am a chicken
and how I don't feel like a chicken
and how I love to run
but I don't want to run
in a herd

and I don't like watching people
worry about fast and faster and fastest
and about
winning and losing

and all the while I am talking
Grandpa is nodding, nodding
and finally he says
You stick to your guns, honey.

And I say
But they say I will regret it—

and Grandpa says
Do you think you will regret it?

And I say
*No—but they think I am wrong
that I can't know
what I will regret.*

And Grandpa says
*Wrong. Right. Regret.
When I stopped running races
everyone told me I was wrong
and everyone told me I would regret it.*

He is looking at the photo of himself
with the trophy.

I ask him
And did you regret it?

Grandpa shifts his gaze to my apple folder.
Not for one tiny minute
he says.

And I want him to say more
to tell me why he stopped running races
but he leans his head back against the chair
and closes his eyes
and falls asleep.

His face looks different in sleep
the muscles slack
the wrinkles smoothed.

Has that brown spot on his cheek
always been that large?
Has it always been the shape
of a pear?

I draw his profile:
the wide forehead
the unruly eyebrows
the noble nose
the downturned mouth.

Is he not happy in his sleep?

I draw the brown spot
and the dimpled chin.

I lie back on the floor
and close my eyes
and try to keep the image
of my grandpa's face
in my mind

and I dream
not of races
but of colored pencils
and charcoal pencils
and thick, white smooth paper
and Grandpa's face. ❖

✳ What can you infer about the relationship between Grandpa and the main character? Which reactions of the characters make you think this?

....

....

....

....

....

....

✳ Find the line where Grandpa says, *Do you think you will regret it?* From that line, what conclusion can you draw about Grandpa?

....

....

....

....

....

....

....

✳ Think about a decision you made. What was the decision? Do you regret it? Explain your feelings about the decision.

....

....

....

....

....

....

....

....

✳ How would you teach some new classmates to make inferences? Explain how making inferences will help them better understand their reading.

....

....

....

....

....

....

....

Notice how characters react to each other. This will help you draw conclusions about their personalities and actions.

You've probably read a story or seen a movie with a mystery in it. People in the story or film look closely at clues. Then they make inferences about what happened. In the same way, you can read about historical events and use clues in the text to make inferences. Your inferences can help you understand what happened and why the events were important.

The Unbreakable Code tells about an important and real event in World War II. In this passage, John's grandfather remembers how he and other Navajo soldiers took part in a top-secret mission for the U.S. military. As you read, underline clues that tell you why the events were important. In the **Response Notes**, write your inferences about the clues. (Remember, an inference is a prediction, a conclusion, or an interpretation.)

from The Unbreakable Code
by Sara Hoagland Hunter

Response Notes

His grandfather began to laugh. "We were known as the toughest platoon at boot camp. We had done so much marching at boarding school that the drills were no problem. Hiking in the desert of California with a heavy pack was no worse than hauling water in the canyon in midsummer. And I'd done that since I was four years old.

"As for the survival exercises, we had all gone without food for a few days. A Navajo learns to survive.

"One weekend they bused us to a new camp in San Diego. On Monday we were marched to a building with bars on every window. They locked us in a classroom at the end of a long, narrow corridor. An officer told us our mission was top secret. We would not even be allowed to tell our families. We were desperately needed for a successful invasion of the Pacific Islands. So far the Japanese had been able to intercept and decode all American radio messages in only minutes. This meant that no information could be passed between American ships, planes, and land forces.

"The government thought the Navajo language might be the secret weapon. Only a few outsiders had ever learned it. Most importantly, the language had never been written down, so there was no alphabet for the Japanese to discover and decode.

"He gave us a list of more than two hundred military terms to code. Everything had to be memorized. No trace of the code could ever be found in writing. It would live or die with us in battle.

"When the officer walked out of the room, I looked at the Navajo next to me and began to laugh. 'All those years they told us to forget Navajo, and now the government needs it to save the country!'

"We were marched every day to that classroom. We were never allowed to leave the building. We couldn't even use the bathroom by ourselves. Each night, an officer locked our notes in a safe.

"The code had to be simple and fast. We would have only one chance to send each message. After that, the Japanese would be tracing our location to bomb us or trying to record the code.

"We chose words from nature that would be easy to remember under fire. Since Navajo has no alphabet, we made up our own.

"'A' became *wollachee*."

"Ant?" asked John in English.

Grandfather nodded.

"'B' was *shush*."

"Bear," said John.

"'C' was *moasi*. 'D', *be*. 'E', *dzeh*." His grandfather continued through the alphabet. Each time he named the Navajo word, John answered with the English.

"We named the aircraft after the birds. The dive-bomber was a chicken hawk. The observation plane was an owl. A patrol plane was a crow. Bomber was buzzard.

"At night we would lie in our bunks and test each other. Pretty soon I was dreaming in code.

"Since we would be radiomen, we had to learn all kinds of radio operations. We were taught how to take a radio apart and put it together in total darkness. The Japanese

fought at night, so we would have to do most of our work in complete darkness. Even the tiniest match flame could be a target.

"When the day came for the code to be tested in front of the top Marine officers, I was terrified. I knelt at one end of a field with our radio ground set. The officers marched towards me. Behind a building at the other end of the field, another code talker sat under military guard waiting for my transmission. One officer handed me a written message:

"'Receiving steady machine gun fire. Request reinforcements.'

"It took only seconds for me to speak into the microphone in Navajo code. The officer sent a runner to the end of the field to check the speed and accuracy of the message. The Navajo at the other end handed him the exact message written in English before he even came around the corner of the building! They tested us over and over. Each time, we were successful. The government requested two hundred Navajo recruits immediately. Two of our group stayed behind to train them. The rest of us were on our way." ❖

✳ Read the sentences in the chart. Write an inference you can make from each sentence. Then explain how your inference helps you understand the mission more fully.

Sentence from the selection	Inference	How does your inference deepen your understanding of the mission?
"We would not even be allowed to tell our families."		
"So far the Japanese had been able to intercept and decode all American radio messages in only minutes."		
"All those years they told us to forget Navajo, and now the government needs it to save the country!"		

✳ Look back at the inferences you wrote in the Response Notes. What new knowledge about World War II have they helped you discover?

....

....

....

....

Making inferences about historical events can help you understand why the event is important.

You may have seen movies or read stories about robots that behave just like humans. Real robots can't do that—not yet. But here's the real question: Would you even want robots to look and act just like people? How would humanlike robots change your world? Making inferences about these questions will help you be prepared for change in the future.

This nonfiction passage is about robots, their relationship with humans, and how they have changed over the years. As you read, underline details that tell about how robots and computers have changed. Write your inferences in the **Response Notes**. (Remember, an inference is a prediction, a conclusion, or an interpretation.)

Response Notes

from **Smart Robots** by Mark Hanlin

Most robots do not look like humans because they do not need to. However, there are human-looking robots working in entertainment parks and amusing customers in shopping malls. Many of these robots appear to be very intelligent, but this is not so. These robots usually have people operating them by remote control from a hidden location. The operator can see and hear the person the robot is talking to via a radio-controlled camera and microphone. The operator can talk back to a person through a speaker on the robot. The sound of the operator's voice is changed by running it through a special electronic box so that the voice sounds as if it has been spoken by a machine. The robot moves around on wheels so the operator can easily control it, like driving a remote-controlled car.

Until very recently, robots usually traveled around on wheels because two-legged robots were very complicated and expensive to make. When robot engineers studied how people walk and balance themselves, they discovered the human body uses many complicated methods. To build a machine to copy this movement and to achieve balance was an awesome task. Not only was a two-legged robot in danger of constantly falling over, but the powerful computer needed to monitor its position and send all the balancing signals was too big to fit on the robot.

The P3 humanoid robot developed by the Honda Corporation has overcome many of the earlier problems associated with two-legged movement. This robot can walk, turn around, and even climb stairs. This is the first step in developing a robot for use around the home.

The P3 still has many limitations. Although it walks on its own, it still has to be told what to do. An operator has to tell it to walk, stop, and climb the stairs. It can operate only in a very limited environment of smooth floors with nothing in the way. It probably could not walk outside, where there are unpredictable obstacles like rocks, strong wind, and loose earth.

For robots like the P3 to be able to operate in a normal human environment, the computers that control them will have to be much smarter. Many people are working on these problems right now in a field called artificial intelligence, or AI.

For many years now, scientists have been trying to make an artificial brain using computers. During the 1950s and 1960s, when computers were first used, people were already calling them electronic brains. Many scientists were convinced that in a few years they would have a computer powerful enough to simulate the human brain. They were wrong. ✣

✳ Reread the second and third paragraphs of the selection. What inference can you make about humans' ability to walk?

....

....

....

✳ Design and draw a robot that would be important and useful in our world. Write about what it would do and why it would be helpful.

....

....

....

....

Making inferences about change can help you be prepared for change in the future.

You probably know a lot about relationships. You're in them with sisters and brothers and relatives and friends. When you read about relationships in stories, you may already be familiar with issues the characters face. Making inferences about these relationships will help you better understand them.

In this passage from the novel *Rules*, you learn about the relationship between Catherine and her autistic brother, David. As you read, look for and underline details that tell about the characters and their relationship. In the **Response Notes**, write inferences you make about their relationship. (Remember, an inference is a prediction, a conclusion, or an interpretation.)

from Rules by Cynthia Lord

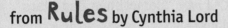

"Come on, David." I let go of his sleeve, afraid I'll rip it. When he was little, I could pull my brother behind me if he didn't want to do something, but now David's eight and too strong to be pulled.

Opening the front door, I sigh. My first day of summer vacation is nothing like I dreamed. I had imagined today warm, with seagulls winging across a blue sky, not overcast and damp. Still, I refuse to grab my jacket from the peg inside the front door.

"Umbrella?" David asks, a far-off stare in his brown eyes.

"It's not raining. Come on. Mom said go to the car."
David doesn't move.
I get his favorite red umbrella.

"Okay, let's go." I step onto the front porch and slide the umbrella into my backpack with my sketchbook and colored pencils.

"Let's go to the video store," David says, not moving one inch.

"You're going to the clinic. But if you do a good job, Dad'll take you to the video store when he comes home."

Response Notes

The video store is David's favorite place, better than the circus, the fair, or even the beach. Dad always invites me to come, too, but I say, "No, thanks." David has to watch all the previews on the store TVs and walk down each row of videos, flipping boxes over to read the parental advisory and the rating—even on videos Dad would never let him rent. David'll say, loud enough for the whole store to hear, "Rated PG-thirteen for language and some violence! Crude humor!" He'll keep reaching for boxes and flipping them over, not even *seeing* the looks people give us. But the hardest part is when David kneels in the aisle to see the back of a video box a complete stranger is holding in his hand.

Dad says, "No one cares, Catherine. Don't be so sensitive," but he's wrong. People *do* care.

Beside me, David checks his watch. "I'll pick you up at five o'clock."

"Well, *maybe* five o'clock," I say. "Sometimes Dad's late."

David shrieks, "Five o'clock!"

"Shh!" I scan the yards around us to see if anyone heard, and my stomach flips. A moving van is parked in front of the house next door, back wide open, half full of chairs and boxes. From inside the truck, two men appear, carrying a couch between them.

My hands tremble, trying to zip my backpack. "Come on, David. Mom said go to the car."

David stands with his sneaker toes on the top step, like it's a diving board and he's choosing whether to jump. "Five o'clock," he says.

The right answer would be "maybe," but David only wants surefire answers: "yes" and "no" and "Wednesday at two o'clock," but never "maybe" or "it depends" or worst of all, "I don't know."

Next door the movers set the couch on the driveway. If I hurry, I can ask them before they head into the house.

"Okay," I say. "Dad will pick you up at five o'clock. That's the rule."

David leaps down the steps just as the moving men climb into the van. He might not understand some things, but David loves rules.

I know I'm setting up a problem for later because Dad's always late, but I have rules, too, and one of mine is: Sometimes you've gotta work with what you've got. ❖

✳ Look back at the details you underlined and the inferences you made. Use these and your Response Notes to write brief descriptions of Catherine and David.

Catherine

David

✳ Draw three conclusions about Catherine and David's relationship. List details that support your conclusions.

Conclusion	Details that support it

✳ How do you think Catherine's relationship with her brother affects the way she sees the world around her?

....

....

....

....

....

....

Drawing conclusions about relationships will help you better understand the characters and their relationships.

8 LESSON

Many of the inferences you make when you read can be applied to other texts or real-life situations. When you read, think about the inferences you are making and what they teach you. These thoughts can stay with you long after you have finished your reading.

As you read this excerpt from the novel *There's a Boy in the Girls' Bathroom,* think about what you learn about Jeff and his situation. In the **Response Notes**, write inferences you make. Consider how you can apply your inferences to other situations.

from There's a Boy in the Girls' Bathroom by Louis Sachar

Jeff Fishkin was hopelessly lost. He clutched his hall pass as he looked down the long empty corridor. The school seemed so big to him.

He was on his way to see the new counselor. She was supposed to help him "adjust to his new environment." Now he not only didn't know how to get to her office, he had no idea how to get back to Mrs. Ebbel's class either.

The floor was slippery. It had started raining during recess and the kids had tracked water and mud inside with them.

A teacher carrying a stack of papers stepped out of a door and Jeff hurried up to her. "Can you tell me where the counselor's office is, please?" he asked. His voice trembled.

The teacher first checked to make sure he had a hall pass. Then she said: "The counselor's office . . . let's see. Go down this hall to the end, turn right, and it's the third door on your left."

"Thank you very much," said Jeff. He started to go.

"No, wait," said the teacher. "That's not right, she's in the new office in the other wing. Turn around and go back the way you just came, then turn left at the end of the hall and it's the second door on your right."

Response Notes

"Thank you," Jeff said again.

He walked to the end of the hall, turned right, counted to the second door on his left, and pushed it open.

A girl with red hair and a freckled face was washing her hands at the sink. When she saw Jeff, her mouth dropped open. "What are you doing in here?" she asked.

"Huh?" Jeff uttered.

"Get out of here!" she yelled. "This is the girls' bathroom!"

Jeff froze. He covered his face with his hands, then dashed out the door.

"THERE'S A BOY IN THE GIRLS' BATHROOM!" the girl screamed after him.

He raced down the hall. Suddenly his feet slipped out from under him. He waved his arms wildly as he tried to keep his balance, then flopped down on the floor.

"Oh no, no, no, oh no, no, no," he groaned. "What have I done? Oh, why didn't I just read the sign on the door? This is the worst day of my whole life!" ❖

✳ Look back at the inferences you made while reading. List two inferences that could be useful in other situations.

Inference	How could this be useful to you in another situation?
Jeff was nervous.	If a new student comes to our school, I'll be extra nice so she doesn't feel too nervous.

✳ What personal connections can you make with Jeff and his experiences?

....

....

....

....

✳ Look over the selections you read for this unit.

■ In which selection did you find it easiest to make inferences? Why?

....

....

....

....

....

....

■ In which selection did you find it most difficult to make inferences? Why?

....

....

....

....

....

....

> Making inferences that go beyond a text will help you create new knowledge.

Synthesizing

Watching football is a lot different from playing it. When you watch a game, you see what happens from the outside. But when you play it, you're much more aware of the details involved in making a touchdown or throwing a pass.

Reading is like playing a sport, too. As an active reader, you're aware of the twists and turns your mind makes. You're on the lookout for new understandings, such as themes, big ideas, and main points the author is trying to make. This process of collecting thoughts, evaluating them, and molding them into new knowledge is called **synthesis.**

In this unit, you'll read about different **journeys** that fictional characters and real people take. You'll practice synthesizing your thoughts to gain a greater understanding of what you read.

When you read, new information may cause you to change or adjust your opinions about a character or an event. This process of changing and evolving thoughts is called **synthesis**.

This selection is from a **biography** of Jim Thorpe, one of the world's greatest athletes. His early school experiences greatly influenced his life. As you read, think about Jim's school. Write your thoughts and opinions about it in the **Response Notes**. Also, look for and underline new information about the school that causes your thoughts to change or evolve.

Response Notes

When did they have time for reading and math?

The teachers sound strict!

from Jim Thorpe by Joseph Bruchac

Thinking back on it, you might say that running was what brought me to football. By that I mean running away from school. After Charlie [Jim's Brother] died, the Sac and Fox Indian Agency School was the last place on earth I wanted to be. I begged to stay home, but Pa said I needed book learning. So back I went.

Book learning. That was far from the only thing I had to do. All of my time at that school wasn't just spent at a desk. They had to keep the costs low and couldn't afford much help. So us students had to do just about all the labor. They had us peeling potatoes, chopping wood and lugging water for the cook, washing our clothes under the watchful eye of the laundress, growing most of the food we ate in the school gardens, mucking out the stables, and cleaning the outhouses.

Now, I was used to hard work. I was glad to do my share of it at home on our ranch. But I resented having to do all those jobs in a school where they never praised you and would just as soon whup you as criticize you. They did plenty of both.

Talk about discipline. Everything there was done by the bell. Whenever that bell rang, you had to move! We got up by the bell, ate by the bell, went to class by the bell, sung the words in *Gospel Hymns* #5 by the bell. And we

didn't just walk from one place to the next, they marched us like stiff little soldiers.

Even playtime—or so they called it—was done by the bell. But we weren't allowed to play the kind of games we all knew as Indian kids. No dart games of mis-qua-pee, or follow the leader or even tag. Instead they made us play horseshoes—probably because it was one game that required us just to stand in one place—until that danged bell rang again. If they could have made us go to the bathroom by the bell they would have done that. To this day, whenever I hear a bell it makes me want to run the other way.

There was about sixty of us, boys and girls. Most of us were Sac and Fox, but there were a few Potawatomis, Kickapoos, Iowas, and even some Ottawas. None of us was that happy to be there. Some of those unhappy children were "blanket Indians" whose families had never spoken English before. Those of us who came from mixed-blood families like mine, where English was spoken, had to act as translators for those boys and girls. We had to tell them that not only had their clothes been taken away and their long hair cut off, but now they didn't even have the same names they came there with. Instead of Chi-ki-ka, she was now Stella. Instead of Keokuk, he was now Robert. ❖

This school was trying to change the kids. I didn't know that at first.

✻ **What were your thoughts about the Sac and Fox Indian Agency School at the beginning of the selection?**

....

....

....

....

....

....

✻ **How did your thoughts about the school change by the end of the selection?**

....

....

....

....

....

....

....

✳ List three important thoughts or insights you have about Jim's school experience. Then use these thoughts to come up with some big ideas about the Indian Agency School.

Three important thoughts or insights about the Indian Agency School

Some big ideas about the Indian Agency School

Notice how new information in a text helps you build new ideas and understanding.

Narrative nonfiction tells a story. It usually contains many of the elements of fiction: setting, characters, conflict, plot, and resolution. When you **synthesize**, it's helpful to focus on one element. Thinking about this one element and how it changes will lead you to a theme or message.

As you continue reading about Jim Thorpe's experience in an Indian boarding school, focus on the conflict and how it develops. The conflict is the discomfort that Jim is feeling. Underline new information you learn about the conflict. In the **Response Notes**, write your thoughts and feelings about the conflict.

Response Notes

My first thoughts about the conflict:

from Jim Thorpe by Joseph Bruchac

We all felt like scarecrows in the clothes they forced us into. We boys wore government issue coats that were made out of thick black cloth. They usually were two sizes too big so we would grow into them. Our heads were weighted down with black felt hats and our necks were strangled with those cheviot shirts with collars as tight as a noose. We even had to wear vests! I was always too hot in those clothes and I couldn't wait to take them off at night. I couldn't hardly imagine how trapped and lost those other kids must have felt. They had grown up on the prairie, wearing soft and comfortable old-style Indian clothes. The kind of "civilization" we had been shoved into must have made them feel like muskrats with their legs in a steel trap.

At night, as I lay in my narrow cot in the boys' dormitory, I could hear some of them crying softly. Now and then, as they slept, I think they'd escape for a time in their dreams. They'd speak out a word or two in our language that made me know they thought they was back home with their families. But if they spoke those words too loud, they might be heard by one of the teachers who monitored us even when we slept. Then they'd be woken up and whupped for talking something other than English. So they couldn't even get away in their dreams.

I felt sad about those "poor uncivilized" boys and girls (as Superintendent Wagner called them), but it was even sadder for me to see their parents. In those days, Indian parents didn't have any choice about what happened to their kids as far as education went. If the government said their children had to go to school, that was it. No explanation, no discussion. The Indian agent would just load them in the wagon and away they'd go.

Those parents had their children taken away from them and couldn't quite understand what this whole school thing meant. Five or six families had followed their children to the school. Since they weren't allowed to stay on the grounds, they had set up camp along the creek by the Sac and Fox Agency so that they could at least see their children now and then. Seeing those sad-faced blanket Indians down by the creek made me miss my own home that much more.

All I could think of was our ranch, twenty-three miles away. It didn't matter if I was sitting in the classroom or working in the harness shop, my heart and my thoughts were at home with Ma and Pa and my little brothers and sisters. I thought of those new colts that needed to be broke. I wondered how the cattle were doing or if the hogs had broken out of their sty again. Maybe there was fence that needed mending. There were twelve hundred acres on our allotment. Pa needed all the help he could get around the ranch.

One day, out of the corner of my eye, I took notice of the fact that my industrial teacher had his back turned. The next thing I knew, I was already halfway home. Of course, like I said before, Pa insisted I had to go back. First he whupped me, just so I would remember what he'd said. Then he hitched the wagon, loaded me in, and drove the twenty-three miles back to the school, where he dropped me off at the gate. But he neglected to tell me I should stay there. As soon as he was over the hill, I took off running across lots. That cut about five miles off the distance home. I got back there just the same time as my father did.

What I'm thinking now about the conflict:

Response Notes

I did that more than once.

"Keep this up, son," Pa said, "and I promise I shall send you so far away to school, you won't be able to run home."

I kept it up and he kept his promise. That was why, in the fall of 1898 when I was just eleven years old, I found myself arriving at the new Haskell Indian Junior College in Lawrence, Kansas. It was 270 miles away from our allotment acres on the North Canadian River, so there was no way I'd be running all that way home. Or so Pa thought. ✥

✳ As you read the passage, how did your thinking about the conflict change? Fill in the chart with your thoughts and with details from the selection.

What I thought or noticed about the conflict in the . . .	Details that influenced my thinking
beginning of the selection:	
middle of the selection:	
end of the selection:	

✳ What decisions did Jim make because of the conflict he felt?

✳ What themes or messages does the author want you to understand about Jim Thorpe and the period in which he lived? To create some themes, use your knowledge of the conflict and along with other information you know.

✳ What is Jim Thorpe's journey?

Follow the changes in one element of text to find an author's theme or message.

When you read, you learn about characters by their words and actions. By studying a character carefully, you can also **synthesize** big ideas the author is trying to get across.

This passage is from *Bud, Not Buddy*, a novel about a boy's experience in the 1930s. As you read, notice Bud's thoughts, words, and actions. In the **Response Notes**, show how your thoughts about Bud change.

Response Notes

What I'm

thinking now:

from Bud, Not Buddy
by Christopher Paul Curtis

Here we go again. We were all standing around in line waiting for breakfast when one of the caseworkers came in and *tap-tap-tap*ped down the line. Uh-oh, this meant bad news, either they'd found a foster home for somebody or somebody was about to get paddled. All the kids watched the woman as she moved along the line, her high-heeled shoes sounding like little firecrackers going off on the wooden floor.

Shoot! She stopped at me and said, "Are you Buddy Caldwell?"

I said, "It's Bud, not Buddy, ma'am."

She put her hand on my shoulder and took me out of line. Then she pulled Jerry, one of the other little boys, over. "Aren't you Jerry Clark?" He nodded.

"Boys, good news! Now that the school year has ended, you both have been accepted in new temporary-care homes starting this afternoon!"

Jerry asked the same thing I was thinking. "Together?"

She said, "Why, no. Jerry, you'll be in a family with three little girls . . ."

Jerry looked like he'd just found out they were going to dip him in a pot of boiling milk.

". . . and Bud . . ." She looked at some papers she was holding. "Oh, yes, the Amoses, you'll be with Mr. and Mrs. Amos and their son, who's twelve years old, that makes him just two years older than you, doesn't it, Bud?"

"Yes, ma'am."

She said, "I'm sure you'll both be very happy."

Me and Jerry looked at each other.

The woman said, "Now, now, boys, no need to look so glum. I know you don't understand what it means, but there's a depression going on all over this country. People can't find jobs and these are very, very difficult times for everybody. We've been lucky enough to find two wonderful families who've opened their doors for you. I think it's best that we show our new foster families that we're very . . ."

She dragged out the word *very,* waiting for us to finish her sentence for her.

Jerry said, "Cheerful, helpful and grateful." I moved my lips and mumbled.

She smiled and said, "Unfortunately, you won't have time for breakfast. I'll have a couple of pieces of fruit put in a bag. In the meantime go to the sleep room and strip your beds and gather all of your things."

Here we go again. I felt like I was walking in my sleep as I followed Jerry back to the room where all the boys' beds were jim-jammed together. This was the third foster home I was going to and I'm used to packing up and leaving, but it still surprises me that there are always a few seconds, right after they tell you you've got to go, when my nose gets all runny and my throat gets all choky and my eyes get all sting-y. But the tears coming out doesn't happen to me anymore, I don't know when it first happened, but it seems like my eyes don't cry no more.

Jerry sat on his bed and I could tell that he was losing the fight not to cry. Tears were popping out of his eyes and slipping down his cheeks.

I sat down next to him and said, "I know being in a house with three girls sounds terrible, Jerry, but it's a lot better than being with a boy who's a couple of years older than you. I'm the one who's going to have problems. A older boy is going to want to fight, but those little girls are going to treat you real good. They're going to treat you like some kind of special pet or something."

How my thoughts
have changed:

Jerry said, "You really think so?"

I said, "I'd trade you in a minute. The worst thing that's going to happen to you is that they're going to make you play house a lot. They'll probably make you be the baby and will hug you and do this kind of junk to you." I tickled Jerry under his chin and said, "Ga-ga goo-goo, baby-waby."

Jerry couldn't help but smile. I said, "You're going to be great."

Jerry looked like he wasn't so scared anymore so I went over to my bed and started getting ready.

Even though it was me who was in a lot of trouble I couldn't help feel sorry for Jerry. Not only because he was going to have to live around three girls, but also because being six is a real tough age to be at. Most folks think you start to be a real adult when you're fifteen or sixteen years old, but that's not true, it really starts when you're around six. ❖

✳ Think about the following excerpts from the selection. What do they tell you about Bud and his experiences? Write your thoughts in the chart.

Excerpt from the selection	What does it tell you about Bud?
"I said, 'It's Bud, not Buddy, ma'am.' "	
"Here we go again. I felt like I was walking in my sleep as I followed Jerry back to the room where all the boys' beds were jim-jammed together."	
". . . I don't know when it first happened, but it seems like my eyes don't cry no more."	
"Most folks think you start to be a real adult when you're fifteen or sixteen years old, but that's not true, it really starts when you're around six."	

✳ Think about what you know about Bud. Combine those details with your own thoughts and experiences to figure out a big idea the author wants you to understand about Bud. This collection of thoughts is your synthesis.

....

....

....

....

✳ What connections can you make with Bud or his experiences?

....

....

....

....

✳ What is Bud's journey?

....

....

....

Thinking about a character's words and actions can lead you to big ideas the author wants you to understand.

....

....

Authors of nonfiction organize their texts in ways that help readers understand the subject. A common text structure that authors use is **cause and effect**. An author will often point out the reasons (causes) why something happens (an effect). Studying cause and effect can help you figure out an author's main idea.

Shipwreck at the Bottom of the World is the true story of the 1914 expedition to Antarctica led by Ernest Shackleton. On this journey, the crew's ship was trapped in a frozen sea for nine months. As you read the passage, look for and underline text where the author uses cause and effect to explain the events. In the **Response Notes**, write thoughts or questions about how your thinking changes.

from Shipwreck at the Bottom of the World by Jennifer Armstrong

Response Notes

Day and night, the men listened to their sturdy ship resist the pressure of the ice. On July 26, the men cheered the return of "Old Jamaica," sailors' slang for the sun. Even its brief appearance raised spirits a little, and by August 1 the pressure on the ship's sides relaxed. The men congratulated one another and praised the ship for withstanding the ice. As August passed in peace and quiet, spirits rose even higher: spring was on the way. Soon the ship would be free, and their journey could continue. All the dogs were brought back on board, in case Dog Town was destroyed by the shifting ice.

But at ten o'clock at night on August 31, the pressure resumed, and the ship began creaking and groaning and trembling like an animal in pain, keeping the men on edge for three days before letting up. September teased them with agonizing on-again, off-again attacks against the ship. Often, it seemed, the pressure coincided with their "gramophone evenings," and some of the more superstitious members of the crew began to think the

music caused the pressure. The gramophone was banned to save argument. An increase in plankton in the water drawn from the boreholes around the ship—a sure sign of approaching spring—didn't ward off the suspense that all the men now felt. The temperature was rising, the sun was shining longer and longer each day, but *Endurance* wasn't free yet.

Worsley noted in his diary on September 22, the first day of the Antarctic spring, "We seem to be utterly abandoned by animal life, and it will be hard with the dogs if we do not get a few penguins soon. The dogs were shedding their winter coats, whining and restless to be off the ship again, and growing hungrier every day.

The afternoon of September 30 brought an enormous ice floe bearing down on the ship from the port side. The floe, which Worsley estimated at possibly a million tons, pressed so hard against *Endurance* that her beams began to buckle and her foremast jerked and shook like a cornstalk in the wind. The attack lasted an hour, leaving the men stunned. In a daze they bent to retrieve the objects shaken from their perches—books, tools, charts, pots and pans, boxes of tea and tins of tobacco, microscopes, clocks, and diaries—and gaped at the bent and buckled decks.

For the next two weeks, the men felt as though they were holding their breath. They hardly dared hope they had seen the last of the pressure attacks. The pack was still drifting steadily northward, carrying *Endurance* with it. The sun was shining almost around the clock, and the temperature had finally climbed above zero. And then on October 18, a misty, gray day, the ice began pressing in again on both sides of the ship.

The ship began to rise to the pressure that was squeezing it up and out of the ice. Suddenly, *Endurance* rolled over onto the port side, and everything that wasn't nailed down slid, slithered, and crashed against the bulwark. Dogs and men all went head over heels in a mass of howling confusion. Some of the men prepared to jump as the ship leaned onto its side, but *Endurance* came to rest at an angle of thirty degrees to port. The pressure stopped again, and the Boss ordered the men to restore order to the jumbled ship. The crew ate dinner that night propped up against the decks like men seated in a grandstand, with their plates in their laps. At eight o'clock, the ship suddenly righted itself again and floated free. *Endurance* had survived another attack. ❖

✳ What are two other important events in the selection that were explained using cause and effect? What big idea can you infer about each event?

Cause	Effect	Big Idea
In July, the sun finally came out.	The men were happy.	They hope the sun will melt the ice so they can finish their journey.

✳ Use the events in the selection along with your previous knowledge and opinions to find a good main idea for this piece. This collection of thoughts is your synthesis.

....

....

....

....

✳ Suppose you were asked to teach another fifth grader about synthesis. How would you explain it? Fill in this chart to organize your thoughts.

What is synthesis?

How do you synthesize?

Why is it important?

Thinking about cause and effect can help you discover an author's main idea.

5 LESSON

A poem can be like a very short story. Each line and detail is important to the meaning of the poem. By thinking about the details and images in a poem, you can **synthesize** big ideas about the piece.

What is goodbye? is a short novel written in verse. Jesse and Jerilyn are brother and sister who are coping with the death of their older brother.

As you read the two poems from the novel, pause often to think about them. Notice where the lines and stanzas end. Think about the details and images you see. Write your thoughts or feelings in the **Response Notes**.

from What is goodbye? by Nikki Grimes

Home Run — Jesse

I was last at bat today.
Our team held two bases.
Pow! I knocked one out of the park.
You should have seen their faces!

I took off around the field,
legs pumping like lightning!
I slid into home plate clean.
Man, I'm so cool, I'm frightening!

There you go, frowning again.
What's the matter, Mommy?
Nowadays, when I have fun,
you lay guilt trips on me.

What am I supposed to do,
spend each minute crying?
I wish I could please you, Mom,
but I'm sick of trying. ✤

Response Notes

✳ How do your ideas and feelings about Jesse change after the first two stanzas?

....

....

....

....

Home Run — Jerilyn

Jesse's eyes flash
a hint of sparkle
not seen since Christmas.
It's his right to smile,
isn't it?
To be delirious?
So what if I don't understand?
This ghost town,
draped in shadow,
is desperate for
a few more watts of light.
A crooked smile, warm as toast,
just might do us all
some good.
Lord knows, these walls
are splattered with
more than enough tears
to go around.
Even the dog is lonely
for the sound
of laughter. ❖

✳ How does Jerilyn's poem help you better understand the family's experience?

....

....

....

....

✳ Use the details from the poem combined with your own thoughts and experiences to synthesize a big idea the author wants you to understand about each child.

Synthesis about Jesse:

....

....

Synthesis about Jerilyn:

....

....

✳ When you're in a bad mood, what do you do to make yourself feel better? Do you call a friend? Listen to music? Take a walk? Write your thoughts below.

....

....

....

....

When you read poetry, think about the details and images to find the big ideas.

An interview with an author (or a poet) often includes questions about the author's childhood and how he or she became interested in writing. By thinking about these details, you can discover some big ideas about the author's life. This process is called **synthesis.**

This selection is from an interview with Nikki Grimes, the poet who wrote *What is goodbye?* that you read in lesson 5.

As you read the interview, notice the details you learn about Nikki Grimes's childhood. Underline details that tell about how she became interested in writing. Write your thoughts about these details in the **Response Notes.**

Response Notes

from An Interview with Poet Nikki Grimes

Q Tell us about your background and what drew you to poetry.

A I started writing poetry when I was six. I just loved language, I loved words. I was fascinated with the notion that one word could mean different things. I would do word games and puzzles and jumbles. I'd go to the dictionary and I'd pick out a word and I'd see all the different words I could make out of it and figure out all the different ways I could use a word.

As for my background, I was born in Harlem and raised in New York City. My first poetry reading was at the Countee Cullen library. They had a poetry reading for young poets and most of them were older than I. My father signed me up for it when I was 13. My first ever. I was shaking in my boots. He just told me to look him in the eye when I was reading. That kind of settled me and I did my first reading.

Q **Where did your encouragement come from?**

A My dad and my sister later on. I lived with her for a few years in my teens. She was embarrassingly supportive. She was the one who would say, "You're gonna hear from this one." She was great. I would wake her up often in the middle of the night, so I could read her a poem that I had written. She never once turned me away. She would rub the sleep from her eyes and sit up and say, "Just give me a minute, Baby."

The way we grew up, she was thrown into the role of mother. She's only four years older than me, but my mother would sometimes leave us alone for two or three days and my sister took charge. I was the baby she took care of.

Q **When you were growing up, did you find books or poems to which you could relate?**

A That was hard. There weren't a lot. No titles even come to mind. Keep in mind, since I grew up in and out of foster homes, I didn't own books. My reading was all in the library—the school library, the public library—and I doubt that I ever read the same book twice. So, I didn't have a favorite author or favorite titles. I just read whatever wasn't nailed down. I would spend hours in the library. When I wasn't there, I was borrowing books. I would take them home, read them, then bring them back. I don't even remember reading a lot of poetry. I remember reading Nancy Drew, Hardy Boys, and myths and legends. I read folktales. I read everything. But when I wrote, it came out in poetry. ❖

✳ **What drew Nikki Grimes to reading and writing? What role did her family play in her writing?**

....

....

....

....

....

✳ **Use the information from the interview along with your previous knowledge to tell the big ideas about why Nikki Grimes became a writer. These ideas are your synthesis.**

....

....

....

....

✳ **Share your syntheses with a partner. Discuss how they're similar or different. How does your partner's synthesis influence your thoughts?**

....

....

The details and images
in an interview can help you
discover a big idea
the interviewer wants
you to understand.

....

....

You can learn about a character by his or her thoughts, words, and actions. You can also learn about a character by what the author says about him or her. By thinking about all the details you know about a character, you can discover big ideas the author wants you to know.

This excerpt is from the novel *Julie of the Wolves*. In it, a young girl named Miyax takes a dangerous journey. As you read, notice Miyax's thoughts and actions. Underline details the author says about Miyax that help create the big picture of who she is. Write your thoughts about Miyax in the **Response Notes**.

from Julie of the Wolves
by Jean Craighead George

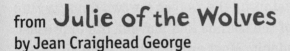
Response Notes

Miyax pushed back the hood of her sealskin parka and looked at the Arctic sun. It was a yellow disc in a lime-green sky, the colors of six o'clock in the evening and the time when the wolves awoke. Quietly she put down her cooking pot and crept to the top of a dome-shaped frost heave, one of the many earth buckles that rise and fall in the cracking cold of the Arctic winter. Lying on her stomach, she looked across a vast lawn of grass and moss and focused her attention on the wolves she had come upon two sleeps ago. They were wagging their tails as they awoke and saw each other.

Her hands trembled and her heartbeat quickened, for she was frightened, not so much of the wolves, who were shy and many harpoon-shots away, but because of her desperate predicament. Miyax was lost. She had been lost without food for many sleeps on the North Slope of Alaska. The barren slope stretches for three hundred miles from the Brooks Range to the Arctic Ocean, and for more than eight hundred miles from the Chukchi to the Beaufort Sea. No roads cross it; ponds and lakes freckle its immensity. Winds scream across it, and the view in every direction is exactly the same. Somewhere in this cosmos was Miyax; and the very life in her body, its spark and warmth, depended upon these wolves for survival. And she was not so sure they would help.

Miyax stared hard at the regal black wolf, hoping to catch his eye. She must somehow tell him that she was starving and ask him for food. This could be done she knew, for her father, an Eskimo hunter, had done so. One year he had camped near a wolf den while on a hunt. When a month had passed and her father had seen no game, he told the leader of the wolves that he was hungry and needed food. The next night the wolf called him from far away and her father went to him and found a freshly killed caribou. Unfortunately, Miyax's father never explained to her how he had told the wolf of his needs. And not long afterward he paddled his kayak into the Bering Sea to hunt for seal, and he never returned.

She had been watching the wolves for two days, trying to discern which of the sounds and movements expressed goodwill and friendship. Most animals had such signals. The little Arctic ground squirrels flicked their tails sideways to notify others of their kind that they were friendly. By imitating this signal with her forefinger, Miyax had lured many a squirrel to her hand. If she could discover such a gesture for the wolves she would be able to make friends with them and share their food, like a bird or a fox. ❖

✳ Write one thought and one action that give you a
sense of who Miyax is and what she's trying to do.
Use your own words.

Miyax's thoughts and actions	What does this tell you about Miyax?

✳ Read the author's words about Miyax below. What do
they tell you about Miyax? Write your thoughts.

Words about Miyax	What do they tell you about Miyax?
"Her hands trembled and her heartbeat quickened, for she was frightened, not so much of the wolves, who were shy and many harpoon-shots away, but because of her desperate predicament."	
"Unfortunately, Miyax's father never explained to her how he had told the wolf of his needs. And not long afterward he paddled his kayak into the Bering Sea to hunt for seal, and he never returned."	

✳ Think of all the details you know about Miyax. Reread the charts on page 201. Synthesize your thoughts to create a brief character description that explains the kind of person she is and the situation she's in.

....

....

....

....

....

....

✳ Share and discuss your character description with a partner. Write one new thought or idea about Miyax that arose from your discussion.

....

....

....

....

....

....

Think about all the details you know about a character to discover the big ideas the author wants you to know.

Nonfiction contains facts and details about a subject. When you read a nonfiction article, you create new understandings by combining the details in the article with the details you already know. You can create new understandings, or **synthesis**, both during and after reading.

As you read this passage from *Top of the World*, underline facts you already know, and circle facts you've just learned. Write questions about the facts in the **Response Notes**.

from Top of the World by Steve Jenkins

Mount Everest is a place of great beauty, adventure, and danger. If you ever want to climb it, here are a few things to think about.

Up and Down
At 29,000 feet, there is only one third as much oxygen as at sea level. In fact, if someone at sea level were suddenly transported to the top of Everest, he or she would die within a few minutes from the lack of oxygen. To prepare for the extremely thin air, you must make several round trips from base camp to higher and higher points on the mountain, sometimes spending the night before starting back down. Staying for increasing periods of time high on the mountain helps keep you from getting altitude sickness.

Avalanche!
When snowfall builds up on a steep mountainside, a whole section of a slope may break loose suddenly and slide down the mountain, moving at speeds of up to 200 miles per hour. More climbers on Mount Everest are killed by avalanches than by anything else.

Hold On
Mount Everest is so tall that it's affected by the jet stream, a narrow, fast-moving air current that circles the world six to ten miles above sea level.

Response Notes

High winds on the mountain make climbing—and surviving—much more difficult. Blowing snow can make it difficult to see, and wind-chill makes the low temperatures feel even colder. The winds are so strong at times that climbers have actually been blown right off the mountain.

Brrr!

The constant cold adds to the challenge of high-altitude mountain climbing. At the top of Everest, typical high temperatures in summer are around -20°F. Nighttime temperatures of -100°F are common. To make matters worse, when there's less oxygen available, it's much harder to stay warm. Well-insulated clothes are a matter of life or death on the mountain.

The Death Zone

Above 26,000 feet, there is so little oxygen that climbers' bodies can't adapt. Anyone who remains at this elevation will get weaker and weaker and eventually die. That's why, once they reach this altitude, climbers have to get to the summit within a day or two. If they don't, they must descend to a lower camp.

The Summit

When you stand on top of Mount Everest, you are the highest thing on earth. For most people, reaching this point is the reward for years of hard work and planning. You can't stay long, though. Your body needs oxygen, which means getting back to a lower altitude quickly. Because you're so exhausted, the descent is one of the most dangerous parts of the climb, so you'll have to be very careful on the way down. ❖

✳ Choose two sections from the article that teach you new facts. Write the names of the sections, the new information you learned, and your new understandings. Your new understandings are your synthesis.

Name of section: Up and Down

New information	New understandings
"...if someone at sea level were suddenly transported to the top of Everest, he or she would die..."	I now understand that air has less oxygen depending on how high up you are.

Name of section:

New information	New understandings

Name of section:

New information	New understandings

✳ Imagine you climbed to the top of Mount Everest. Write a detailed diary entry telling about your experience. Include facts, details, and new understandings from the selection.

✻ Describe what's happening in your mind when you synthesize information.

....

....

....

....

✻ How does synthesizing information make you a better reader?

....

....

....

....

✻ Whose journey from this unit will be most memorable for you? Why?

....

....

....

....

....

To create new understandings, combine new information with facts you already know.

accompanied joined; followed

allotment the amount allowed

ambled walked casually

anemone a circular sea animal rimmed with wavy feelers, or tentacles

artificial human-made

asking questions a reading strategy in which the reader asks questions about what he or she wants to know about a text

assailant one who attacks

associated thought of as connected

astonishment surprise; amazement

avalanche a mass of falling snow or rocks down the side of a mountain

awnings shades that stick out from fronts of buildings

barbed wire fence wire with sharp points

barren without life

biographical sketch a brief history of a person's life and accomplishments

bondage slavery

bulwark a wall used for defense

bureaucratic having to do with the government

cacophony a clashing combination of sounds or colors

caribou reindeer, a large deer

caseworkers people in charge of social-work cases

cattle drive leading cows to another place far away

cause and effect the ways in which an event (cause) brings on another event (effect)

cavalry soldiers on horseback

characterization the way an author develops the people, animals, and imaginary creatures in a story

charred burned to charcoal

chum chopped fish thrown overboard to attract larger fish

civilization ways a culture believes people should live

component a part

consciousness awareness

contracted pulled up

cosmos a vast space

counselor person who helps people with their problems by listening and giving advice

crude offensive; rude

debris garbage

defect to leave

delirious overly excited

depression a time when many people are poor

depressions indentations

desperate having lost hope

dialogue a conversation between two characters in a story

digestive tract intestines

discern to understand or realize

dread fear

edible can be eaten

elevation height

embers hot ashes that contain fire

engulfing taking over

epidemic the rapid spreading of an infectious disease throughout a population

escorted guided or brought

executive order law issued by the President

expectant eagerly awaiting something

FBI the Federal Bureau of Investigation, a national police force

federal having to do with the U.S. government

floe an iceberg

foremast the forward mast on a ship

foster home a place where a child lives temporarily when he or she cannot live with his or her own family

free verse poetry that does not contain regular rhyme or rhythm

futile useless, producing no result

ghost town a small city where people no longer live

gramophone machine that plays music

grant give

grit sand

harpoon a large barbed spear with a rope on it

headings titles of sections in nonfiction pieces

historical fiction made-up stories that are based on events that really happened

hospitable welcoming

hovered stayed in one place in the air

hull the part of a ship that sits below water

humor when an author uses funny events or words to express important ideas or to amuse the reader

images mental pictures created by a reader as he or she reads

initiated started

inoculated injected with a weakened form of a disease to protect against the disease

insistent determined

instruct teach

intercept get something before it reaches its intended destination

interview a direct way to learn about a person by asking him or her questions

invasion entrance by force

jabbed poked

keg line a fishing line attached to the side of a boat

kin person or people related to you; family

lamented expressed grief about

larvae infant, wormlike forms

laundress a woman who washes clothes

limitations things that keep something or someone from doing something

lugging carrying

luxurious expensive and comfortable

main idea a central point that the author wants you to know about a topic

making inferences a reading strategy that involves finding unstated meaning by putting together something you have read with something you know from real life

making connections a reading strategy that involves comparing what you are reading to something you already know

manacled handcuffed

matted tangled and pressed down

melodious having a pleasing tune

merged came together

mesa flat hill with steep sides

mess hall large dining room

mis-qua-pee a Native American dart game

modest plain

mucking cleaning

mute silent

narrative nonfiction a true piece of writing that tells a story

notion idea

novelty something unusual

P

perches sits

pesticides chemicals used to destroy organisms that harm plants

pillars posts

pivotal a turning point

plateau area of high, flat land

point of view how one sees an event; perspective

potential possibility

predicament a troublesome situation

prediction an educated guess, based on background knowledge and story clues, about upcoming events in a text

primer an easy reading book

primitive not modern

priority first and most important thing to do

profile someone's face seen from the side

protective gear outerwear that protects a person from cold and wet

protested spoke out against

psychologist someone trained to counsel people

pulpit a rail at the bow of a boat to protect the person fishing from being pulled overboard

puny small, unimportant

pupae intermediate forms of an insect, between the larval stage and the adult stage

pursed gathered or wrinkled

R

reaps gathers (the crops); gets (the reward for work done)

rebelled acted against

recruits people asked to join the military

refugee a person who escapes danger or persecution

regal like a king or queen

regret sadness about something done or not done

reined pulled on the reins

reinforcements additional people or troops

remote far away from everything

S

scaffolding wooden platform

scrunches pinches

scuttled ran in quick small steps

sensory images language and details that appeal to the reader's five senses

sensitive bothered by what other people think or say

sentimental expressing feelings, often in a "sappy" way

serene happy and calm

shan't the contraction of shall not

shrieks cries out with piercing sound

simile a technique of figurative language in which the characteristics of one thing are described in terms of something else using the words *like* or *as*

simulate act like

singed burned the edges

skeptically doubtfully; unbelievingly

skiff boat small enough for one person to row or sail it

slogged walked slowly, usually through something wet

smolder burn slowly without flames

social service benefits or government funds available for those in need

solemnly very seriously

specific nouns words that name objects in a very clear way

stalactites drippings from lime and water that look like icicles and hang in caves

stock-in-trade what someone is known for

summit the top

superintendent boss of a school or organization

superstition a belief not consistent with known facts or logical thought

supportive encouraging

surefire can be counted on to be right

synthesis the process of collecting thoughts, evaluating them, and molding them into new knowledge

T

taking notes a way to organize ideas by making short written comments about what one is reading

tentacles long, flexible feelers

theme a story's central message

tinged slightly colored or flavored

tittered laughed lightly

tolerated put up with

toxic poisonous; causing severe illness or death

transmission the act of being sent, as in a message

treacherous dangerous

tremble shake

tyrants cruel rulers

ultimately in the end

uncivilized behaving in a way that does not fit the culture

university college

unpredictable unexpected; not behaving in an expected way

unruly hard to control

utter total

visualize to create mental images of what you read

wake ripples in the water made by a moving boat

wing a side section that is separate from the main building

8 "The Street Sweeper" from *A Piece Of The Wind* by Ruthilde Kronberg and Patricia C. McKissack. Reprinted by permission of the author.

16, 20 From *The Young Man And The Sea* by Rodman Philbrick. Scholastic Inc./Blue Sky Press. Copyright ©2004 by Rodman Philbrick. Reprinted by permission.

25 From *The American Story* by Jennifer Armstong and Roger Roth, illustrator, copyright ©2006 by Jennifer Armstrong. Illustrations copyright ©2006 by Roger Roth. Used by permission of Alfred A. Knopf, an imprint of Random House Children's Books, a division of Random House, Inc.

28 From *Artist In Overalls* by John Duggleby. Copyright ©1995. Reprinted with permission of Chronicle Books.

32 From *Esperanza Rising* by Pam Munoz Ryan. Scholastic Inc./Scholastic Press. Copyright ©2000 by Pam Munoz Ryan. Used by permission.

36 From *Dr. Jenner And The Speckled Monster: The Search For The Smallpox Vaccine* by Albert Marrin, copyright ©2002 by Albert Marrin, text. Used by permission of Dutton Children's Books, A Division of Penguin Young Readers Group, A Member of Penguin Group (USA) Inc., 345 Hudson Street, New York, NY 10014. All rights reserved.

39 from *Love That Dog* by Sharon Creech. Copyright ©2001 Reprinted with permission by HarperCollins.

42 "The Pasture" *from The Complete Poems Of Robert Frost* by Robert Frost. Copyright ©1969 Reprinted by permission of Henry Holt and Co.

44 "Jake's Plea", from *Remember The Bridge: Poems Of A People* by Carole Boston Weatherford, copyright ©2002 by Carole Boston Weatherford, text. Used by permission of Philomel Books, A Division of Penguin Young Readers Group, A Member of Penguin Group (USA) Inc., 345 Hudson Street, New York, NY 10014. All rights reserved.

48 "B.B. King" from *The Blues Singers: Ten Who Rocked The World* by Julius Lester. Copyright ©2001 Reprinted by permission of Hyperion Books.

52 From *This Land Was Made For You And Me* by Elizabeth Partridge, copyright ©2002 by Elizabeth Partridge, text. Used by permission of Viking Penguin, A Division of Penguin Young Readers Group, A Member of Penguin Group (USA) Inc., 345 Hudson Street, New York, NY 10014. All rights reserved.

56 Excerpt from *The Voice That Challenged A Nation: Marian Anderson and the Struggle for Equal Rights* by Russell Freedman. Copyright ©2004 by Russell Freedman. Reprinted by permission of Clarion Books, an imprint of Houghton Mifflin Company. All rights reserved.

60 From *Mistakes That Worked* by Charlotte Foltz. Illustrations by John O'Brien, copyright ©1991 by Charlotte Foltz Jones. Used by permission of Random House Children's Books, a division of Random House, Inc.

63 From *Stolen Dreams* by David L. Parker with Lee Engfer and Robert Conrow. Copyright ©1998 by David L. Parker. Reprinted with the permission of Lerner Publishing Group, Inc. All rights reserved. No part of the text excerpt may be used or reproduced in any manner whatsoever without the prior written permission of Lerner Publishing Group.

70 from *Iqbal* by Francisco D'Adamo, translated by Ann Leonori. Copyright ©2001 Edizioni El. English translation copyright ©2003 Ann Leonori. Reprinted with the permission of Atheneum Books for Young Readers, an imprint of Simon & Schuster Children's Publishing Division.

74, 76 "The Golden Touch: The Story of Bacchus and King Midas" from *Favorite Greek Myths* by Mary Pope Osborne. Scholastic, Inc. Text copyright ©1989 by Mary Pope Osborne. Used by permission of Brandt & Hochman Literary Agents, Inc. Any electronic copying or distribution of this text is expressly forbidden. All rights reserved.

80 From *Tsunami* by Ann Morris and Heidi Larson. Copyright ©2005 by Ann Morris and Heidi Larson. Reprinted with the permission of Lerner Publishing Group, Inc. All rights reserved. No part of the text excerpt may be used or reproduces in any manner whatsoever without the prior written permission of Lerner Publishing Group, Inc.

84, 87 Excerpt from *Lincoln: A Photobiography* by Russell Freedman. Copyright ©1987 by Russell Freedman. Reprinted by permission of Clarion Books, an imprint of Houghton Mifflin Company. All rights reserved.

90, 94 "Chapter Eleven" from *Miracle's Boys* by Jacqueline Woodson, copyright ©2000 by Jacqueline Woodson, text. Used by permission of G.P. Putnam's Sons, A Division of Penguin Young Readers Group, A Member of Penguin Group (USA) Inc., 345 Hudson Street, New York, NY 10014. All rights reserved.

98 From *After The Spill* by Sandra Markle. Copyright ©1999. Reprinted with permission by Walker Publishing Co.

03 From *My Life As A Fifth Grade Comedian* by Elizabeth Levy. Copyright ©1998 Reprinted by permission of HarperCollins.

107 From *Meet Famous Latinos: Mario Molina - Interview*. Published on teacher.scholastic.com. Copyright ©2007 by Scholastic Inc. Reprinted by permission.

112 "Aquarium" by X.J. Kennedy, from *Carnival Of Animals: Poems Inspired By Saint-saens' Music*. Copyright ©2006 Published by Candelwick Press, reprinted with permission by the author

116 "Letter from a Concentration Camp" by Yoshiko Uchida, copyright ©1990 by Yoshiko Uchida, from *The Big Book For Peace* edited by Ann Durell and Marilyn Sachs. Used by permission of Dutton Children's Books, A Division of Penguin Young Readers Group, A Member of Penguin Group (USA) Inc., 345 Hudson Street, New York, NY 10014. All rights reserved.

120, 123 From *A Small White Scar* by K.A. Nuzum. Copyright ©2006 Reprinted by permission of Joanna Cotler Books, an imprint of Harper-Collins.

127 From *Free Baseball* by Sue Corbett, copyright ©2006 by Sue Corbett. Used by permission of Dutton Children's Books, A Division of Penguin Young Readers Group, A Member of Penguin Group (USA) Inc., 345 Hudson Street, New York, NY 10014. All rights reserved.

131, 134 Reprinted with the permission of Atheneum Books for Young Readers, an imprint of Simon & Schuster Children's Publishing Division from *Beetles, Lightly Toasted* by Phyllis Reynolds Taylor. Copyright ©1987 Phyllis Reynolds Taylor.

138 Reprinted with the permission of Atheneum Books for Young Readers, an imprint of Simon & Schuster Children's Publishing Division from *Let Me Play* by Karen Blumenthal. Copyright ©2005 Karen Blumenthal.

144, 148 From the book *True Tales Of Animal Heroes* by Allan Zullo, published by Scholastic in 2005© The Wordsellers, Inc.

152 From *The Great Fire* by Jim Murphy. Copyright ©1995 by Jim Murphy. Reprinted by permission of Scholastic Inc.

155 "Grandpa Talk" from *Heartbeat* by Sharon Creech. Copyright ©2004.

160 From *The Unbreakable Code* by Sara Hoagland Hunter. Copyright ©1996. Reprinted by permission of Northland Publishing.

164 From *Smart Robots* by Mark Hanlin. Copyright ©2003.

167 From *Rules* by Cynthia Lord. Scholastic Inc./ Scholastic Press. Copyright ©2006 by Cynthia Lord. Reprinted by permission.

171 From *There's A Boy In The Girls' Bathroom* by Louis Sachar, copyright ©1987 by Louis Sachar. Jacket art copyright ©1987 by Richard Williams. Used by permission of Random House Children's Books, a division of Random House, Inc.

178, 182 From *Jim Thorpe:* Original *All-American* by Joseph Bruchac, copyright ©2006 by Joseph Bruchac. Used by permission of Dial Books for Young Readers, A Division of Penguin Young Readers Group, A Member of Penguin Group (USA) Inc., 345 Hudson Street, New York, NY 10014. All rights reserved.

186 From *Bud, Not Buddy* by Christopher Paul Crutis. Copyright ©1999 Reprinted by permission of Random House Inc.

191 From *Shipwreck At The Bottom Of The World* by Jennifer Armstrong. Copyright ©1998. Reprinted by permission from Crown Publishers, a division of Random House.

195 From *What Is Goodbye?* by Nikki Grimes. Copyright ©2004. Reprinted by permission of Hyperion.

198 Excerpt from an interview with Poet Nikki Grimes from "Language Arts", Vol. 84, No. 3, January 2007, pp. 281. Copyright ©2007 by the National Council of Teachers of English. Reprinted with permission.

201 pp. 5-7 from *Julie Of The Wolves* by Jean Craighead George. Copyright © 1972 by Jean Craighead George. Used by permission of HarperCollins Publishers.

204 Excerpt from T*he Top Of The World: Climbing Mount Everest* by Steve Jenkins. Copyright ©1999 by Steve Jenkins. Reprinted by permission of Houghton Mifflin Company. All rights reserved.

ILLUSTRATIONS

3 –7, 15, 47, 79, 111, 143, 175: Marci Roth; **21 *c*:** © Colin Newman/Dorling Kindersley RF/Getty Images; **55 *t,b*:** Chris Lensch; **58, 59 *tr*:** Helen Dardik; **100:** Geoff McCormack; **124:** Micha Archer; **166:** Chris Lensch; **193 *t*, 194 *t*:** Shadra Strickland
All additional art created by AARTPACK, Inc.

PHOTOGRAPHY

Photo Research by AARTPACK, Inc.

Cover, 1: © Milan Chuckovich/Stone/Getty Images; **8:** © timur1970/Fotolia; **9:** © Image Source/Getty Images; **10:** © Rob Marmion/Fotolia; **11:** © Adam Gryko/Fotolia; **12:** © Graça Victoria/Fotolia; **13:** © Diane Diederich/istockphoto; **13:** © Mark Rasmussen/Fotolia

Introduction 8: © timur1970/Fotolia; **9:** © Image Source/Getty Images; **10:** © Rob Marmion/Fotolia; **11:** © Adam Gryko/Fotolia; **12:** © Graça Victoria/Fotolia; **13 *t*:** © Diane Diederich/istockphoto; **13 *b*:** © Mark Rasmussen/Fotolia

Unit 1 16: © Comstock Images/Jupiterimages; **17 *t*:** © Comstock, Inc.; **17 *b*:** © Open Door Images/Jupiterimages; **18 *t*:** © C Squared Studios/PhotoDisc Green/Getty Images; **18 *l*:** © Colin Newman/Dorling Kindersley RF/Getty Images; **18–19 *b*:** © DAJ/Getty Images; **20:** © Creatas/Inmagine; **21 *b*:** © Bruce W. Heinemann/PhotoDisc/Getty Images ; **23 *t*:** © Martina Berg/Fotolia; **23 *b*:** © Creatas/Inmagine; **24:** © Jim Parkin/Fotolia; **25:** © Corbis; **26:** © Pictorial Press Ltd/Alamy; **27:** © Digital Vision Royalty Free Photograph/Inmagine; **28:** © Christie's Images/Corbis/© Estate of Grant Wood/VAGA, New York; **29:** © Ric Ergenbright/Corbis **30:** © Jim Reed/Corbis; **32:** © Kamil Vojnar/Workbook Stock/Jupiter images; **33:** © Photowood Inc./Photowood Inc./Corbis; **34:** © Sonya Etchison/Fotolia; **35 *t*:** © PhotoDisc/Getty Images; **35 *b*:** © Darrell Gulin/Corbis; **36:** © Bettmann/Corbis; **37:** © Time Life Pictures/Getty Images; **38 *r*:** © Hemera Technologies/Jupiter Images; **38 *l*:** © Comstock, Inc.; **39 *bl*:** © Elenathewise/Fotolia; **39 *br*:** © Boris Kaulin//Fotolia; **39 *t*:** © Brandxpictures/Inmagine; **40:** © PhotoDisc/PhotoDisc Blue/Getty Images; **41:** © James Nazz/Corbis; **42:** © Paul Steinmann/Fotolia; **43 *b*:** © Corbis/Jupiter Images; **43:** © marilyna/Fotolia; **44 *t*:** © Keren Su/Corbis; **44 *b*:** © John Foxx/Stockbyte Silver/Getty Images; **45:** © PhotoDisc/Getty Images; **46:** © Izzy Schwartz/PhotoDisc/Getty Images;

Unit 2 48: © Associated Press/Keystone, Martial Trezzini; **49 *c*:** © Tom Perkins/Fotolia; **49 *b*:** © Tom Perkins/Fotolia; **50:** © Lanny Ziering/Brand X/Corbis; **51 *r*:** © Tim Mosenfelder/Corbis; **51 *b*:** © Tom Perkins/Fotolia; **52:** © Associated Press; **53:** © Corbis **54:** © Robert Glusic/Corbis; **55:** © PhotoDisc/PhotoLink/Getty Images; **56:** © Bettmann/Corbis; **57:** © Bettmann/Corbis; **59:** © Fabrizio Bensch/Reuters/Corbis; **60:** © Jim Craigmyle/Corbis; **62 *r*:** © Lorcan/Digital Vision/Getty Images; **62:** © Comstock, Inc.; **63:** © John Van Hasselt/Corbis Sygma; **64:** © Corbis; **65:** © Ivan Khafizov/Fotolia; **66:** © John Van Hasselt/Corbis Sygma; **67:** © Robert Glusick/PhotoDisc/Getty Images; **68:** © Michele Falzone/JAI/Corbis; **69:** © Christine Osborne/Corbis; **70:** © John Van Hasselt/Corbis Sygma; **72:** © John Van Hasselt/Corbis Sygma; **73:** © Tina Rencelj/Fotolia; **74:** © Arte & Immagini srl/Corbis; **75:** © Look and Learn/The Bridgeman Art Library; **76:** © 2007 Jupiter Images; **77:** © Darren Greenwood/Design; **78:** © Carson Ganci/Design Pics/Corbis Images;

Unit 3 80: © James Pomerantz/Corbis; **81:** © Warren Bolster/PhotoDisc/Getty Images; **82:** © Punit Paranjpe/Reuters/Corbis; **83:** © Warren Bolster/© PhotoDisc/Getty Images; **84:** © Brooks Kraft/Corbis; **85:** © Bettmann/Corbis; **86:** © R Morley/PhotoLink/PhotoDisc/Getty Images; **87:** © George Eastman House/Hulton Archive/Getty Editorial; **88:** © Carlin Photo/istockphoto; **89:** © grivet/Fotolia; **89 c:** © Comstock, Inc.; **90:** © Stuart Brill/istockphoto; **91:** © John Rich; **93:** © Tobbe/zefa/Corbis; **94:** © Robert Morris/Alamy; **95:** © Gg/Jupiter Images; **96:** © Brooklyn Production/Corbis; **97 t:** © Crystal Kirk/Fotolia; **97 c:** © Comstock, Inc.; **97 b:** © Jack Hollingsworth/Corbis; **98:** © PhotoDisc/Getty Images; **99:** © Digital Vision/Getty Images; **101:** © PhotoDisc/Getty Images; **102:** © Kaz Chiba/PhotoDisc; **103:** © Leah-anne Thompson/Fotolia; **104:** © Bloomimage/Corbis; **105:** © Bloomimage/Corbis; **106 t:** © Tetra Images/Corbis; **106 c:** © Comstock, Inc.; **107:** © AP Photo/Steven Senne; **108:** © J. Emilio Flores/Corbis; **109:** © InterNetwork Media Inc./PhotoDisc/Getty Images; **110:** © Tom Stewart/Corbis

Unit 4 112 t: © Hal Beral/Corbis; **112 b:** © Macduff Everton/Corbis; **113 c:** © Kees Opstal/Fotolia; **114:** © Comstock, Inc.; **114** cheetah: © 2007 Jupiter; **114** boy: © Bob Thomas/Corbis; **115:** © PhotoDisc/Getty Images; **116:** © Corbis; **117:** © Corbis; **119:** © Liubov Vadimovna/Fotolia; **120:** © Steve Mason/PhotoDisc Green/Getty Images; **121:** © Edmond Van Hoorick/PhotoDisc/Getty Images; **122:** © Edmond Van Hoorick/PhotoDisc/Getty Images; **123:** © Glow Images/Alamy; **125:** © Thinkstock/Corbis; **126:** © Kelly Redinger/Design Pics/Corbis; **127:** © Najlah Feanny/Corbis Saba; **128:** © Alley Cat Productions/BrandX/Corbis; **129 r:** © Mikhail Basov/Fotolia;

129 l: © Mikhail Basov/Fotolia; **130:** © Kaz Chiba/PhotoDisc/Getty Images; **131:** © Harutaka Nodera/MIXA/Getty Images; **132:** © 2007 Jupiter Images; **133:** © Gregor Schuster/zefa/Corbis; **133 t:** © Undine Freund/Fotolia; **133 b:** © Jose Luis Pelaez, Inc./Corbis; **134:** © David R. Frazier Photolibrary, Inc./Alamy; **135:** © Altrendo Images/Altrendo/Getty Images; **136:** © imagebroker/Alamy; **137:** © Kaz Chiba/PhotoDisc/Getty Images; **137 t:** © John-Francis Bourke/zefa/Corbis; **137 b:** © Undine Freund/Fotolia; **138:** © Lucy Nicholson/Reuters/Corbis; **139:** © Bettmann/Corbis; **140:** © Dimitri Iundt/TempSport/Corbis; **141:** © Comstock, Inc.; **141 t:** © Corbis; **142:** © Shaun Botterill/Getty Images

Unit 5 144: © Purestock/Getty Images; **145:** © Con Tanasiuk/Design Pics/Corbis; **146:** © Jeff Vanuga/Corbis; **147:** © Hemera Technologies/Jupiter Images; **148:** © Michael S. Quinton/National Geographic/Getty Images; **150:** © Andy Fyon; **151:** © Bruce Heinemann/PhotoDisc/Getty Images; **152:** © ivp/Fotolia; **153:** © Bettmann/Corbis; **154:** © Alloy Photography/Veer; **155:** © Freddy Smeets/Fotolia; **156:** © TongRo Image Stock/Jupiter Images; **157:** © Victoria Short/Fotolia; **158:** © Digital Vision; **159:** © Digital Vision; **160:** © Corbis; **161:** © Jose Gil/Fotolia; **162:** © Corbis; **164:** © Haruyoshi Yamaguchi/Corbis; **165:** © Gregor Schuster/zefa/Corbis; **167 tr:** © Stockbyte/Getty Images; **167** rain: © Alexander Wurditsch/Fotolia; **168:** © JackSullivan/Alamy; **169:** © Jack Hollingsworth/Corbis; **170:** © surflifes/Fotolia; **171:** © Jim/Bastardo/Stone/Getty Images; **172 bl:** © Vast Photography/Jupiter Images; **172 br:** © Vast Photography/Jupiter Images; **173:** © Donna Day/Photodisc/Getty Images; **174:** © image100/Corbis